"*Surviving God*, by Grace Ji-Sun Kim and Susan M. Shaw, is a monumental gift to the church and to survivors alike. With profound insight and theological precision, Kim and Shaw reexamine the Scriptures from the point of view of the God who survives, survivors in the Scriptures, and Jesus—the survivor of sexual violence. *Surviving God* is both indictment and healing balm for the church in an age of reckoning."

—**Lisa Sharon Harper**, critically acclaimed author of *The Very Good Gospel* and *Fortune: How Race Broke My Family and the World—and How to Repair It All*

"Kim and Shaw courageously address the difficult reality of sexual assault and violence in both society and church. The authors' multilayer approach includes their dialogue with each other, as well as stories from other survivors of sexual abuse. Even in a world of suffering and injustice, this book provides a helpful method of critique and reimagination that presents pathways to new understandings and practices, with the potential for new hope and joy."

—**Edwin David Aponte**, dean of the Theological School and professor of religion and culture at Drew University

"*This book is for survivors*. It is a theological life preserver for victims of sexual harm and abuse and for anyone who has inherited warped images of God from patriarchal systems. *Surviving God* exposes the toxic theology that dominates much of evangelical Christianity, but more importantly, it exchanges those distortions for images of God that offer hope and comfort. Grace and Susan's engagement with Scripture, the church, and the experiences of sexual survivors is as unflinching as it is healing. Their writing is catalytic—from the multifaceted theological perspectives and keen cultural insights they give to the courageous vulnerability they and other survivors show in their poetry and testimonies.

"*But this book is not only for survivors*—it is for those who have forced others to become survivors through their abuse, rejection, silencing, and neglect. If I were in charge, I would make this required reading for the leaders of every church that has swept abuse under the rug, allowed enabling structures to harm the vulnerable, or failed to believe and support victims in their congregations. *Surviving God* is a gift to survivors of all kinds and a call to repentance and action to everyone else."

—**Jennifer Garcia Bashaw**, associate professor of New Testament and Christian ministry, Campbell University

"How can we transform rape culture? By reimagining our society's all-powerful, authoritarian, male God. Centering the voices of sexual abuse survivors, *Surviving God* shows us a path through the dark thicket of a violent God, toward the sunlight of a God who yearns for justice and joy."

—**Christa Brown**, author of *This Little Light: Beyond a Baptist Preacher Predator and His Gang*

"This timely, powerful book radically centers the experiences of sexual abuse survivors. It addresses with sensitivity the tensions of negotiating a faith tradition that has compounded abuse, yet also simultaneously offers visions of a more just community. The authors do not let God off the hook, but acknowledge that God, too, can be understood as a co-survivor of, and escapee from, toxic theologies."

—**Susannah Cornwall**, author of *Constructive Theology and Gender Variance* and *Un/Familiar Theology*

"Surviving God: A New Vision of God through the Eyes of Sexual Abuse Survivors is a much-needed message of assurance and comfort for survivors of sexual abuse and those who support them. As survivors themselves, Grace Ji-Sun Kim and Susan M. Shaw made the hard journey of deconstructing their learned theology and reimagining God as one who suffers with us, liberates us for the work of justice, and calls us to create beloved communities that are safe, welcoming, liberatory, and transformative. In these days of never-ending sexual-abuse news stories, both in and outside the church, *Surviving God* is an important word for faith leaders and survivors."

—**Rev. Dr. Pamela R. Durso**, president,
Central Seminary, Shawnee, Kansas

"In *Surviving God*, Grace Ji-Sun Kim and Susan M. Shaw offer critical and life-giving perspectives, as well as urgently needed theological language, to dismantle the images of God that perpetuate violence and offer in their place a kaleidoscope of images, metaphors, and concepts of the divine that not only speak to the suffering of those who have experienced sexual violence but provide a pathway toward realizing beloved community. Theology done through the eyes and voices of survivors of sexual violence and abuse is something that every community that calls itself Christian needs."

—**Mary Foskett**, chair, Department for the Study
of Religions, Wake Forest University

"*Surviving God* is about sexual abuse, traditional Christianity, and the powerful, undeniable, and excruciating connections between the two. The book interlaces its challenging theological and biblical work with painful, evocative stories, poetry, and reflections on sexual abuse by the authors and others they interviewed. The chapter on Jesus as a likely sexual abuse victim was devastating and yet, in the end, offers believers another reason to love him and to seek to co-create alongside this suffering one a world where no one is ever again abused. I cannot say that this was a fun read, or that I agreed with every theological or exegetical suggestion. I do say, with all my heart, that *Surviving God* is an essential book for everyone who cares about the suffering of the innocent and the moral worthiness of this religion called Christianity."

—**David P. Gushee**, author of *Changing Our Mind*, *After Evangelicalism*, and *Defending Democracy from Its Christian Enemies*

"*Surviving God* is an empowering read for survivors and those struggling to overcome pain, despair, and anguish from sexual abuse and assault. This is an excellent resource book for individuals, churches, and communities seeking to end sexual violence and moving toward healing and wholeness."

—**Rev. Jesse Jackson Sr.,** president and founder of Rainbow PUSH Coalition and author of *Keeping Hope Alive*

"For anyone longing for an understanding of God beyond the toxic and abusive theologies of the patriarchy—this book is for you! *Surviving God* is a courageous act of 'indecent theology' that witnesses to the complexity of the divine and guides readers in recovering, reimagining, and reclaiming God from the violence of hateful theology."

—**Rev. Dr. Rebecca Todd Peters**, professor of religious studies and founding director of the Poverty and Social Justice Program at Elon University, and author of *Trust Women: A Progressive Christian Argument for Reproductive Justice*

"More than bad acts perpetrated by a few 'bad apples,' sexual violence involves intersecting dynamics that include centuries of Christian thought, practice, and imagination. In this powerful book, Kim and Shaw expose the ways Christian theology enables sexual abuse in church and world. They also offer an empowering Christian theological vision of survival. Drawing on biblical narratives, theologies, and divine images of survival, *Surviving God* invites its readers to walk with the Jesus who suffers and survives with all people."

—**Tracy Sayuki Tiemeier**, professor and chair of theological studies, Loyola Marymount University, Los Angeles

Surviving God

A NEW VISION OF GOD

THROUGH THE EYES OF

SEXUAL ABUSE SURVIVORS

SURVIVING
GOD

GRACE JI-SUN KIM AND
SUSAN M. SHAW

Broadleaf Books
Minneapolis

SURVIVING GOD
A New Vision of God through the Eyes of Sexual Abuse Survivors

Copyright © 2024 Grace Ji-Sun Kim and Susan M. Shaw.
Published by Broadleaf Books, an imprint of 1517 Media. All
rights reserved. Except for brief quotations in critical articles
or reviews, no part of this book may be reproduced in any
manner without prior written permission from the publisher.
Email copyright@1517.media or write to Permissions,
Broadleaf Books, PO Box 1209, Minneapolis, MN 55440-1209.

"Jesus in Abu Ghraib," by Pádraig Ó Tuama taken from *When
Did We See you Naked? Jesus as a Victim of Sexual Abuse* by Jayme
R. Reaves, David Tombs and Rocio Figueroa Alvear published
by SCM Press is copyright © The Editors and Contributors
2021 and is reproduced by permission. All rights reserved.
rights@hymnsam.co.uk

Library of Congress Control Number: 2023025892 (print)

Cover design: Olga Grlic

Print ISBN: 978-1-5064-9578-1
eBook ISBN: 978-1-5064-9594-1

Dedicated to

All survivors of sexual assault and abuse,
as well as those who did not survive

Contents

PREFACE

Let's begin by introducing ourselves:

Grace: I was born in Korea, immigrated to Canada, and now teach in the United States. Immigration to Canada in 1975 wasn't easy as we had to deal with racism every day. Many made fun of us and called other immigrant kids who looked like me racial slurs like "Ching-Chong," "Jap," and "Chink." Even though we did not speak English well, we all knew that these were not compliments but slurs intended to make fun of who we are.

Our family, like many Korean immigrants, turned to the church to make friends, find employment, teach Korean culture and language to the second generation, and share a place of cultural engagement. Our family became dedicated churchgoers, and church took over our social lives. At the same time as I experienced racism at school and in society, I experienced sexism in the church. During difficult moments of racial discrimination and gender oppression, I often wondered where God was and how I worshipped a God who seems to allow racism and sexism to exist and persist. To answer these questions, I went to Knox College at the University of Toronto and got my MDiv and then gained my PhD in theology at the University of St. Michael's College. Getting my degrees was the beginning of my theological journey.

I struggled with the male image of God, patriarchal theology, and white European theology, and this led me to engage with liberation theology, feminist theology, and Asian American theology. It is in tackling these issues that I can finally write about sexual abuse in the church and how we are to deal with this pressing issue theologically, biblically, and spiritually.

Susan: I grew up in Georgia in a fundamentalist Southern Baptist church. Our family was the kind who went to church "every time the doors were open." I learned to take the Bible seriously, and because of that, by the time I was in high school I had begun to question my church's literalist reading of the Bible. Being a college English major opened up even more questions as I became a close and critical reader of texts. After college, I went to the Southern Baptist Theological Seminary in Louisville, Kentucky, at that time a theologically moderate seminary, thinking I'd spend my life serving Southern Baptists as a writer and editor. During my time there, I encountered enough men telling me women didn't belong and enough moderate-to-progressive theology that I became a feminist and decided to become a professor. Teaching religion in conservative Christian liberal arts colleges, however, turned out to be a difficult, if not impossible, task for a young feminist who was just starting to come out of the closet. So, I did what any good scholar does during a life crisis: I went back to school. This time I got a master's in what was called "women studies" at the time, and my mentor offered me a job at Oregon State University. I taught everything from feminist theories to women and sexuality, to gender, race, and pop culture, while I kept one foot in the world of academic religion, writing about Baptist women and theology and teaching courses in feminist theologies and feminism and the Bible.

In fact, that's how we met. Susan was using one of Grace's books in her feminist theologies class. A colleague told Susan that he'd communicated with Grace and asked if Susan would like him to see if Grace would come speak at Oregon State. Of course, Susan agreed enthusiastically. We immediately hit it off, and for years talked about doing a project together, but we didn't know what, and each of us had other projects to complete. Finally, in 2013, we both had time and an idea that became our first book together, *Intersectional Theology: An Introductory Guide*. This book centers an idea from feminist theories—intersectionality, the concept that explains how social differences like race and gender shape one another and our experiences within systems of power and privilege—in doing theology. We so enjoyed working together that we decided we wanted to do another project, and that's where the idea for this book started.

We both survived childhood sexual abuse. We also survived God, at least the God of our childhood churches. That God willed abuse, or at least allowed it, and then judged us for letting ourselves be abused. We had to survive that God, even long after the abuse ended, while we still held onto those images of God that had enabled our abuse.

Later we learned that God doesn't cause or will or want abuse—any kind of abuse. Rather, God suffers with us; God survives with us. God is a surviving God who experiences our suffering and is with us in our pain.

For many survivors, God also has to survive some pretty harmful ideas that make abuse even worse. These ideas may lead survivors to walk away, rejecting any idea of God at all because they can't reconcile what happened to them with the notion of a divine being, especially a loving and just divine being.

The church has told us that women and girls are temptresses, that sexual minorities and transgender people are inherently disordered and sinful, that women and children are supposed to submit to the men in power over them, that survivors have to forgive their perpetrators, and that perpetrators don't need to make restitution for their abuse. Many survivors have internalized these ideas to their own detriment. After all, the church doesn't generally encourage us to ask hard questions. For many survivors, holding onto faith is difficult because churches have often taught ideas of God that are thoroughly tied up with experiences of abuse, and the church and individual Christians have often failed to take abuse seriously and do something about it. When someone is abused by a priest, a man who is supposed to stand in God's stead, continuing to believe in a loving God is almost impossible. It's also hard to stay committed to the institution of the church when the church covers up the abuse, moves the abuser onto another church, and tells the victims they're lying or delusional or unfaithful.

For many survivors, there comes a time when old answers and patriarchal understandings of God no longer work. There's a break, a point of no return, when we say, "That's it. If that's who God is, then I guess I'm done with God." We each reached a moment in our own journeys when the God of our childhoods no longer aligned with our experiences of a God of love and justice. We realized we could not hold onto the idea that God controls everything and that somehow our abuse was part of a divine plan. In fact, we came to see that the very notion that God causes or allows sexual abuse is pretty ungodlike in itself. It is a belief that enables abuse and keeps structures of power and violence in place. Healing the soul-wounds of abuse requires new images of God that can comfort, nourish, sustain, and empower. For ourselves as survivors, we've had to rescue the image of God from patriarchal theologies that are soul-murdering, abusive, and subordinating. We've had to reimagine images of God from our own places as survivors. For each of us, God had to survive really bad theologies that nearly broke our faith in order for God's love and justice at last to shine through. This process of critique and reimagination is what we more fully develop in this book and one we hope helps our fellow survivors on their journeys of healing and enables allies and churches to be more informed, supportive, and engaged.

When we decided to call our book *Surviving God*, we liked all the possible meanings of the title. We think it captures how we've had to survive the God of our childhoods and youth, and the God of bad ideas that marginalize and oppress; it also includes how God has survived with us as God has suffered with our suffering; it also notes how God has survived the harmful beliefs that alienate us from God. We hope that you will join us in our journey of surviving God and moving toward liberation, freedom, and joy.

In the context of much of Christian thinking, God is an all-powerful being who controls the world. This is a God who wills or allows abuse, a God we must survive, the terrifying God of our childhoods. When we see God this way, we have no choice but to lay some of the blame for our abuse at this God's feet. God caused it, or God allowed it. Either way, God is culpable. God is complicit in sexual violence.

In the following chapters, we want to dismantle the God we must survive, the violent God who participates in sexual violence. These images of a violent God have deep roots, all the way back into the Bible's First Testament. As we'll see, however, these images have also served a purpose that's not so godly—they've kept powerful and abusive men in power. These images have become the basis for beliefs that have justified and excused sexual violence right down to our present day. These images continue to perpetuate abuse and harm survivors. In the first few chapters, we'll take a look at these images from the perspectives of survivors, and we'll explore why they're problematic and what harm they do.

Next, we'll offer alternative ways of imagining a God who survives with us. This God empowers us to liberate ourselves and work for justice for all people and calls us to move the church toward a beloved community that is safe, welcoming, liberatory, and transformative. This God is the source of our hope that keeps us working toward change. This God wants us to live flourishing lives filled with love and joy.

These reflections aren't top-down, coming from church hierarchies or pastors who tell survivors what to believe. Instead, our process begins with survivors and asks how we can understand God through their (and our) eyes. We talked with other survivors, and sometimes you'll hear their voices directly. We tell our own stories as well, and these are woven throughout the book. From these various experiences and perspectives, we scrutinize what we've traditionally been taught about God, and we consider what we might learn by thinking about God through the lenses of survivors.

While we started this book before the COVID-19 pandemic sent us all into lockdown, the past three years' experience reminds us why rethinking God is so important. During lockdown, the rates of gender-based violence soared. The increased stress of the pandemic and economic precarity, along with the enforced proximity of lockdown, meant many women and children were at increasing risk of violence, with few options for escape. Also, during this time, we continued to learn of powerful Christian men who had used their positions of trust and respect to prey on women and children, and we saw how ineffective, if not downright complicit, churches were in addressing abuse.

The ways we think about God are rooted in experience in conversation with Scripture, tradition, and culture. In traditional theologies, the experiences of elite white men predominate and are assumed to apply to everyone else. After all, historically speaking, elite white men are the ones who have had the power and resources to write theology. In this book, however, we begin our thinking about God in the particular experiences of victims of sexual violence and abuse. We rely both on our own experiences and on the experiences of others who've written about or talked to us about their own experiences. We refer to "victims" and "survivors" throughout the book. There's no agreement about the best language to use. For some people, "survivor" connotes a positive reclamation of life after abuse; others feel the word diminishes the ongoing struggles to survive because of the continuing impact of sexual violence. Some people prefer "victim" to underline the violence done to them by perpetrators; other people do not at all want to be seen as victims. We use both terms to recognize that many of us have survived gender violence, and yet we still suffer from its effects, and some of us do not survive.

In our earlier book, *Intersectional Theology*, we argue that all the ways we think about God should be intersectional. Intersectionality is an idea that arose from the ways Black feminist theorists have thought about how their experiences of sexism and racism are inseparable, interrelated, and intertwined. Intersectionality is a lens for analyzing the ways social categories such as gender, race, social class, sexual identity, ability, nationality, and age shape people's experiences within larger structures of power and social institutions such as government, education, the family, and the church. That means that we think about God from our own perspectives, which are shaped by our experiences of gender, race, class, and other differences, and, importantly, we recognize and include those perspectives that are different from our own in order to have a fuller, more comprehensive view of God. We also pay attention to how our identities situate us in relation to power. Power is a shape-shifter that changes across contexts. While we both experience discrimination as women, in some denominations neither of us would be welcomed to preach. Susan doesn't have to worry that her race as a white woman will work against her if she applies for a new position or is nominated for an award. Grace, however, as a Korean American woman, knows that racial stereotypes about Asian women mean white male students may expect her to be more accommodating to them than their white professors. On the other hand, Grace is never excluded by a church because she's married to a man. Many churches, however, would not welcome Susan, who is married to a woman.

As another example, when gender-based violence happens to Black women and girls, it always happens within a context of racism. Within white supremacy, Black women and girls are targeted in specific ways by white perpetrators whose interlocking notions of gender and race see Black women and girls in particular dehumanized and sexualized ways. Additionally, Black women and girls experience violence at the hands of Black men whose gendered rage is shaped by their own sense of powerlessness within the system of racism.[1] Responses to gender-based violence, then, must address these intersections. Supporting survivors and ending gender-based violence against Black women and girls requires engagement with larger efforts of struggle and resistance to white supremacy.

Here's yet another example: Korean comfort women were usually impoverished teenagers when the Japanese army kidnapped them and forced them into sexual slavery during World War II. Their experience of gender-based violence became a wound for the entire nation. Only in 1991 did the first comfort woman make her experience public, beginning a movement that demanded full disclosure by the Japanese and reparations for comfort women. Healing for comfort women required the public telling of their stories and official recognition of their suffering. Yet Japan's 2015 apology hardly rose to the level of repentance necessitated by the atrocities of sexual slavery during war. Still, the fact of this level of gender-based violence raises questions, not only about our political systems but also about God's presence in the world, sin, suffering, redemption, and justice.

Thinking about God should be a liberatory task, one that addresses both personal faith and social justice. Theologies of liberation recognize that the call of the gospel is to change the world as well as to change individual lives. Our thinking about God, therefore, should move us toward those goals, helping us support individual people and make structural changes in the world that address injustice, discrimination, and oppression. For example, in the past few years, we've seen primarily Christian involvement in attempting to pass bills that would prevent transgender people from using the bathroom that matches their gender identity. Some Christian leaders have argued that allowing "men" in women's bathrooms puts women and girls in danger, and yet we know that transgender women in particular are at great risk of gender-based violence and murder. Some Christians believe that God has ordained two genders with separate and complementary roles. They also believe that God has ordained a hierarchy of gender that makes men leaders and women subordinates. Transgender people violate these norms about gender and represent a threat to the gender hierarchy these beliefs uphold. In 2017, a group of Catholic bishops issued a letter reiterating the gender binary and calling for public policy to keep the two genders intact.[2] Survivors of sexual violence, however, can help us think differently about the gender binary and about gender hierarchies. Survivors have experienced directly and traumatically the impact of theologies that reinforce gender norms and gendered power, and privileging their perspectives helps us see the world and God from fresh angles.

As we think about surviving sexual violence, we find places where we can learn from survivors, and we recognize that survivors have unique locations from which to teach us new things about God. Survivors come from different places; have different experiences based on gender, race, class, sexuality, ability, age, and nation; have been part of different Christian traditions; and experience sexual violence differently. That means any attempt to build our thinking about God from surviving sexual violence must be attentive to these differences and recognize how different locations and experiences contribute to different viewpoints and ideas. While we engage in this task from our own identities, we also look to other survivors to inform, broaden, and deepen our thinking in this book.

Surviving sexual violence has lasting negative impact and continues to send ripples across survivors' lives long after the violent experience itself. By centering survivors in our thinking about God, we can begin to ask important questions about how we understand God in the midst of sexual violence, how sexual violence shapes how we think about human nature, how we must reimagine redemption, especially for the perpetrator, how we come to grips with the church as an institution that has facilitated harm and as a community that is called to love and heal survivors and perpetrators, and how we envision a future in the midst of harm and devastation.

Many perpetrators have distorted understandings of God which often provide internalized legitimacy of their horrid, violent acts. Survivors too carry these images that intensify their shame and guilt. Churches accept, reinforce, and promote beliefs and images that protect perpetrators and make survivors responsible for their own abuse. That is why this book is important. In these pages, we issue a direct challenge to Christian beliefs that position women as subordinate and submissive as a condition of God's divine wisdom. We take issue with human and divine violence and churches and family structures that rely on and perpetuate gender-based violence. We contend that a God who causes or allows abuse and sexual violence is unacceptable and false, and we call on Christians to do better in confronting the pervasive problem of sexual violence. Such a task means getting rid of old and often dangerous metaphors like God as Father or King and creating new images helpful in processes of healing and dismantling sexual violence. We look to biblical survivors for wisdom, and we explore the usefulness of seeing Jesus himself as one who experienced sexual violence.

As outrageous as it sounds, the problem of sexual violence is pervasive in the Christian church. In fact, we'd go so far as to say the church enables a culture of sexual abuse through many of its beliefs and practices. The problem of sexual abuse is larger than the proverbial "few bad apples." Instead, we think a big part of the problem has to do with what many Christians believe about God and how those beliefs have been created and shaped by men with power to keep men in power.

Often, we don't even think of our images of God as images. We think of them as concrete realities. We turn them into idols. And, so, for example, when we think God is a master, we think God really is a white overlord who has the right to control and discipline and use violence. This image also reminds us of how important it is to keep intersectionality—the ways gender, race, and other kinds of difference shape each other—central in our thinking. In addition to traditional Christian thinking about God, other traditional Christian ideas can be especially problematic for survivors. Two "troubling" beliefs in particular create difficulties for many survivors within the context of Christian faith—forgiveness and submission. Traditional ideas about forgiveness say survivors should forgive their perpetrators and move on, and notions of submission make women vulnerable by telling them they should do what men in authority tell them to do.

Additionally, when we imagine God as male, we often assume human males are more godlike and have godlike power over girls and women. We believe women should submit to men like we submit to God. We buy into negative depictions and stereotypes of women like the ones we find in purity culture that tell us women are responsible for men's sexuality, and, if men engage in sexual sin, it's girls' and women's fault. We also learn from the Bible that God is violent. God punishes, strikes, and kills people. God's violence then justifies men's violence.

These beliefs harm survivors and make healing more difficult by shaming and blaming girls and women who internalize these ideas. In this traditional way of thinking about God, God is one more thing victims have to survive.

Fortunately, these violent images and troubling beliefs aren't the only possibilities within Christian faith. Many images of God can be encouraging and healing for survivors and the church. While often traditional images of God fail by simply reinforcing abuse, images that arise from survivors' experiences offer alternatives that show God as healing, mothering, relating, providing, and overcoming. These images of God let survivors see themselves reflected in a God who shares their experiences and imagine a God who understands their pain and grief. These images also reveal a God who loves unconditionally and who nurtures and restores.

The Bible is also filled with people who survive (and many who don't) sexual violence. When we read these stories from intersectional feminist perspectives, we can think about these "texts of terror" and "texts beyond terror" in ways we don't usually hear in Sunday school. These readings are exciting and imaginative ways to rethink old patriarchal interpretations of the Bible that may enable sexual abuse and excuse violent behavior. In the ways we read these stories, in the best of liberation traditions, we find God as the one who sides with people victimized by sexual violence and who demands justice for them.

We furthermore discover Jesus himself as a survivor of sexual violence. At his crucifixion, Jesus was stripped naked as a way to humiliate him. Given what we know about Roman crucifixion, we can also assume Jesus was sexually assaulted as part of his torture. When we read the story this way, Jesus becomes not a judge but a fellow sufferer with survivors of sexual violence. Instead of focusing on Jesus as a victor, we recognize Jesus as a victim and a survivor. The crucifixion is not some part of God's divine plan to save humanity but rather an inevitable consequence of Jesus's challenge to the social and political order of his day. The resurrection is God's affirmation of Jesus's decision to use love instead of power and to demand justice for the most marginalized. Jesus's survival is hopeful for survivors of sexual abuse because we see that God affirmed Jesus as a survivor.

We too can be resurrected and transformed through embodied mindfulness. Too often, abuse splits survivors' minds from their emotions and their bodies, yet joy comes to us through the integration of these different aspects of self. God intends joy for all of us, and that joy can be found in the struggle for human liberation from oppression.

We work within a tradition of liberative theologies that center the experiences of the marginalized and give preference to the vulnerable, the poor, the outcast, the victim. In shifting the center, we bring to light both overt and subtle problems of sexual violence in Christian thinking and practice, and we offer insights toward constructing more inclusive and useful understandings of God that validate, support, and help heal survivors.

The question for us is not what a belief is but rather what it does. Does it make us kinder? Does it make us more loving? Or does it justify our violence, our uses of power, and our hierarchies? For us, surviving God means deconstructing old notions that are part of the problem of sexual violence and imagining new ways of thinking about God that help us heal and be better people in the world. The Surviving God we call on in this endeavor is not the Violent God of so much Christian thought and history, but the God who, too, has suffered and who works alongside us in the world to end sexual violence and suffering.

CHAPTER 1

Trust and Obey

The God of our childhoods was terrifying. Sure, He (and it was always "He") loved us, but we also knew He could destroy us in a moment if we displeased Him. Poof! Like Lot's wife, we'd become a pillar of salt. God knew us intimately and had complete control over us. Like an abuser, He asked us to love Him even as He threatened us with the torments of hell if we didn't.

We were told not to question Him; we were to submit and obey. Our metaphors—Father, Master, Lord, and King—reinforced this, and we were to submit and obey in the same way to the men who stood in God's place for us—fathers, pastors, husbands, teachers, leaders. The very words we used to describe God—almighty, powerful, all-knowing, majestic, righteous—instilled fear in us as they underlined the sense that God could do to us whatever He wanted at any time, for any reason. And we were to thank Him for it.

Week after week we heard the stories—Miriam stricken with leprosy, Sapphira falling down dead at Peter's feet. We memorized the Bible verses: "Behold, I set before you this day a blessing and a curse. A blessing, if ye obey the commandments of the Lord your God, which I command you this day. And a curse, if ye will not obey the commandments of the Lord your God." "Wives, submit yourselves to your husbands, as unto the Lord." "Obey them that have the rule over you, and submit your-selves." We even sang it—"Perfect submission, perfect delight"; "I surrender all"; "Trust and obey"; "Have thine own way, Lord, have thine own way. Hold o'er my being absolute sway."

Everywhere we turned we were told to submit and obey—God, fathers, pastors. The message became part of us. Good girls, good boys, and good women did as they were told and kept quiet about it.

What a setup for abuse.

Susan: I grew up a fundamentalist Southern Baptist. We believed God was in control of everything. God didn't cause everything, but everything happened either in the perfect will of God or in the permissible will of God. Nothing that happened, then, was outside the will of God. Human freedom came in being able to choose to act within either the perfect or permissible will of God. Really, only after my abuse ended and I began to reflect on it as a young adult did I come to find this aspect of our fundamentalist faith to be problematic. During my abuse, I could not even have imagined asking questions of this notion of God. I was too busy blaming myself. Somehow, I thought, I needed to make the abuse stop, and so my prayers asked God to forgive me for not stopping the abuse. I know that sounds unbelievable now, but that is the logic of fundamentalism.

Only as a young adult in seminary did I find a place to ask the hard questions of this picture of God: If God is a God of love, why did God allow this to happen to me? Is there any lesson so important that God could only teach it to me through abuse? If God could have stopped this and didn't, what kind of God is that? Fundamentalism could provide no answers that satisfied me. "We can't know the mind of God" or "God has 'His' purposes" simply no longer worked for me. I decided that there was no lesson I needed to learn that was so valuable that abuse was the only way I could learn it and that, if God could have stopped the abuse and didn't, then that was no God I needed to love. That God was involved in the abuse, an abuser Himself. These realizations left me with no alternatives within fundamentalism. I had to reimagine God, to discover a God who did not control the world, who could not have stopped the abuse, and who suffered with me. I also as a feminist had to come to the conclusion that suffering is not redemptive and that making suffering noble simply assures that suffering will continue.

Grace: As I grew up as a child of an immigrant, the Korean Pres-byterian Church was very important to our family. Our immi-grant life was enmeshed and intertwined with church and all it had to offer. God was viewed as the almighty Father God who has full control over everything, even our own lives. God is powerful, masculine, and a "Father" to all of us on earth. I had some prob-lems with this patriarchal image of God while growing up in the church. I was trying to figure out how to reconcile an almighty Father God with an image of a loving God who nurtures us and cares for us. When I was being sexually abused, I could not comprehend what was happening to me. I was young and didn't understand the evilness of sexual abuse. It was a tormenting time as I didn't know how to reconcile a God who loves us with a God who allows such things to happen.

As I grew up, I then had to deal with the consequences of being abused, and the psychological and theological torment was enormous and overbearing. Sexual abuse feels out of your control when you are a young girl, and I questioned my childhood under-standing of an all-powerful and almighty Father God. I believed that an almighty God would not allow such violent acts to occur. During this tumultuous time, I cried out to God Father almighty whom I believed had full control over all things, and prayed that the abuse would stop. As much as I cried, nothing happened. Since God didn't stop the abuse, I started to slowly question the God of my upbringing. My whole understanding of God—an under-standing taught to me at the conservative Korean Presbyterian Church—was falling apart.

My ongoing questions about the nature and image of God led me to pursue a degree at a seminary in hopes of unpacking the God that I worship. My studies led to questions like: Which God do I worship? Is it the Father almighty God who is all powerful yet doesn't stop abuse? Or do I worship a loving Spirit God who is present in our pain, suffering, and even abuse, helping us to a fuller and deeper understanding of God?

Both of us have struggled to reconcile what we were taught by the church and what we experienced as abused children. We've not only survived our abuse; we've survived the abusive God of our childhood and the churches that forced images of a violent God upon us. We take the language, images, texts, and rituals of the church seriously, and as feminists we bring an intersectional lens to our exploration of the Divine: that is, we recognize that our own gender, ethnicities, sexual identities, physical and mental abilities, social class, education, and ages play a role in how we think about and experience God. We also know we need to hear the experiences and perspectives of people who differ from us to have a fuller understanding of God. As we suggested in our book *Intersectional Theology*, our thinking about God is kaleidoscopic, always changing, always tentative. Our reflections offer one piece of this kaleidoscopic image, and we hope they encourage others to add their own stories and understandings to create a richer, fuller picture of the God who survives.

Telling Indecent Stories

Our method for exploring how sexual abuse affects our images and offers new visions of God begins in storytelling—in telling indecent stories, the stories of our abuse. Argentinian feminist theologian Marcella Althaus-Reid says that indecent stories problematize layers of oppression. They question the traditional order of "decency." They require theological and sexual honesty, and they offer a challenge to dominant stances.[1] The stories of survivors are indecent—they are stories that uncover and undress injustice. They are indecent because we are not supposed to tell them. But as poet Audre Lorde explains, our silence will not protect us.[2]

The crucifixion and resurrection are indecent stories because they uncover abuse and injustice, and they affirm God's siding with the oppressed. Jesus died because he challenged the dominant religious, ethnic, cultural, class, and, yes, sexual norms of his day. He was a threat to empire because his loyalty to God outweighed his loyalty to Caesar, and he was a threat to religion because his embodied faith refused to be constrained by laws that were inhumane in their application.

The resurrection was Jesus's coming out. His surviving of the abuse of the cross vindicated his love for everyone, a love without boundaries of nation, religion, ethnicity, or gender. Survivors of sexual abuse, too, have resurrection stories, those indecent stories of living through abuse, speaking out, and challenging the people and institutions that have failed survivors.

The resurrection shattered social, political, and religious norms. Jesus suffered at the hands of the power systems of his day, but, in his resurrection, God came out on the side of the oppressed and marginalized. God stood alongside those who suffer. God announced the end of the decent, moral order of the day that crushed anyone who was different, who refused to bow down before unjust power. Survivors understand resurrection. As ones who have suffered unjustly under interlocking systems of sexism, racism, classism, ableism, and heterosexism, we understand what it means to refuse our invisibility, to suffer for claiming our full humanity, and to be resurrected in living honestly and bravely in love.

Our stories of surviving expose the structural inequities that constrain and threaten our lives. They help us see where transformation is needed. They call out for justice. Here is another indecent story from the Gospel of Luke:

> In a certain city there was a judge who neither feared God nor had respect for people. In that city there was a widow who kept coming to him and saying, "Grant me justice against my opponent." For a while he refused; but later he said to himself, "Though I have no fear of God and no respect for anyone, yet because this widow keeps bothering me, I will grant her justice, so that she may not wear me out by continually coming." (Luke 18:2–5)

Our stories, like the widow's, are a cry for justice. Her story is indecent because this woman who meant little within the structures of judicial power still prevailed by her persistence and by her refusal to be defined by stereotypes and ideologies outside herself. This widow is indecent because she demanded the right to be heard, the right to be treated as a full human being. Her cry for justice is ours.

Not all of survivors' stories are stories of suffering and injustice. Many of our stories also show us all the resurrections we've already experienced. They are the indecent stories of our surviving and thriving. Every story of surviving is a story of resurrection. Every challenge to abuse is a resurrection story. Every story of loving and laughing and getting through another day is a resurrection story. From these indecent stories we critique dominant and oppressive images of God, and we offer alternative images, better images, that affirm love over power, healing over abuse, and welcome over violence.

#MeToo and #ChurchToo

In 2017, courageous women set off a virtual firestorm when they started to tweet about their abuse within the church: "When I was 16 years old I was groomed for abuse by a man in his early 30s who was a 'youth leader' in my evangelical megachurch." With this tweet in November of that year, Emily Joy Allison launched a Twitter conversation that soon she and friend Hannah Paasch named #ChurchToo. Within hours, thousands of tweets came in with other people telling their stories of sexual abuse within the church.

> I was raped when I was 9 by a member of my church. The pastor, and my parents, told me I needed to forgive him, as that is what Jesus would do. They made me hug my rapist and tell him I forgave him.

> A teacher and an esteemed member of the baptist [sic] church I grew up in was caught with a student. 4th grade. Others

came forward. The church protected him. My best friend was one of his victims. She committed suicide in HS.

From 15–17, I was groomed, groped, kissed, manipulated by a married man within the Christian community. It's been 20 yrs. It's still difficult to talk about it because purity culture taught me it was my fault, and still scared I'd be blamed if I spoke up.

About a month before this, actor Alyssa Milano had tweeted, "If you've been sexually harassed or assaulted write 'me too' as a reply to this tweet." Within two days, #MeToo had been used 825,000 times, and within twenty-four hours, nearly five million people on Facebook responded to #MeToo, with over twelve million posts, comments, and reactions. This movement built on previous work by activist Tarana Burke, who had started "Me Too" on Myspace a decade earlier to help young girls of color deal with the trauma of sexual harassment, abuse, and assault.

Susan: #MeToo. I didn't tweet it. But I could have. I was sexually abused as a child. Even now, that sentence is hard to write. It was the 1970s. We didn't talk about those things back then. I understood that what was happening to me was wrong. And I knew I had to keep it to myself, even as people believed my abuser was a good Christian man. I lived with my shame in silence. I never told anyone what happened to me until I was in my early twenties. As a professor of women, gender, and sexuality studies I talk about these things all the time now. Even so, writing this book pushes me beyond my comfort zone because Grace and I have chosen to make this book personal. I don't know how else we begin to repair the damage to ourselves and to our relationships with the church and with God until we speak the truths of our lives. Feminists have long said the personal is political, and so our stories are one starting point for our struggle with God and our struggle for liberation for all people from the structures that continue to facilitate abuse and harm.

Almost immediately, the #MeToo movement had freed many women and other people to tell their stories of sexual harassment, abuse, assault, and rape. Then, with Emily Joy's post in November 2017, #ChurchToo reminded us that the Christian church itself was also a place with a long and sordid history of gender-based violence that has continued into the present. We had already by this time learned of the sex abuse scandal in the Catholic Church, though survivors are still uncovering the unimaginable scope of that betrayal. On #ChurchToo, we heard stories of teenage girls raped by evangelical youth pastors, gay teens shamed to suicide, children abused by churchgoing fathers, wives beaten by men in church leadership, victims told to forgive their perpetrators or to ask God for forgiveness for their part in their own sexual assault. We began to understand the lengths to which churches would go to protect beloved pastors and other men in authority and how deeply they would bury survivors' stories and pain under a layer of God-talk. And even though we are aware that survivors need to heal from their experiences, we may not have recognized how deeply their experiences impact the ways they think about God. We know some have left the church. Some have lost their faith in religious institutions altogether. And for some, their experiences cause them to ask deeper faith questions: how can we understand God, think about sin (both individual and collective), grapple with Jesus and the cross, make sense of redemption for both victims and perpetrators, and envision a more equal future?

Grace: As a child, I was sexually abused and the shame of abuse kept me silent. I dared not tell anyone, as I am Asian American and the culture of honor/shame among Korean Americans meant I could not speak about what had happened to me lest I bring shame on myself and my family. This culture of honor/shame still guides our behaviors and our conversations in the Asian American culture here in North America. Thus, even though I experienced sexual abuse, I could not tell anyone. I was terrified of the shame that I would experience, as if I were the cause of the sexual abuse. Therefore, I kept it to myself, and it was an added burden and pain that I couldn't speak. It was not until the middle of my Master of Divinity program at Knox College that I finally told someone of my painful experience of sexual abuse and how it continued to hurt me every day. The damage was real, and I felt the pain as if it had just happened at the present moment. This is the reality of sexual abuse. The pain lasts a long time, and it just doesn't seem to go away.

Sexual Violence Has Lasting Effects

While we were still reeling from #MeToo and #ChurchToo, along came the confirmation hearing for Supreme Court nominee Brett Kavanaugh. Professor Christine Blasey Ford alleged Kavanaugh had assaulted her at a party when they were teenagers. Reactions to the hearing fell along familiar lines and highlighted the difficulties of coming forward to tell stories of gender-based violence. Blasey Ford was accused of lying, of being part of a plot, of waiting too long. However, false accusations make up only a small fraction of the total, and innocent men almost never face criminal charges (much less get convicted or serve time). In fact, false allegations are usually made by young women who are trying to avoid punishment, have become pregnant (in which cases, the *parents* usually make the accusation), who need medical help of some kind, or who have other complicating factors that make their lives chaotic.[3] Christine Blasey Ford hardly fits this description. Neither do most survivors.

For many survivors of sexual violence, the Kavanaugh hearing was hard, triggering painful memories and feelings, and retraumatizing them.

Susan: I feel mostly healed from my experiences. Rarely are they more than an emotional blip for me. Yet the Kavanaugh hearing brought the hurt and rage roaring back. Watching people question

> *Blasey Ford's story reminded me why I didn't say anything back in the 1970s. I was a child. I feared what would happen if I said something. Most of all, I feared no one would believe me. I couldn't watch the hearing. I started watching The Great British Bake-Off instead. Something about run-of-the-mill Brits baking biscuits and pastries I'd never heard of, even as they cried and hugged the baker who had to leave the show at the end of each week, calmed me. I even started baking myself. For the first time in my life, I threw myself into biscotti and soda bread, and I found peace elbow deep in dough.*

Survivors have all kinds of reactions to their trauma. Some bake. Many become anxious or depressed. Some develop eating disorders, PTSD, suicidal thoughts, substance abuse, and/or self-harm. Many change their routines, stop participating in activities, withdraw from their communities, change schools or drop out entirely, move out of their residences, and/or change or quit their jobs. Many spend years in counseling.

Some suppress their experiences of abuse, hoping that they can forget it and just move on with their lives. Unfortunately, suppressing past experiences of sexual abuse rarely works as these memories often surface in later stages of survivors' lives, and other incidents may trigger these memories. Furthermore, some don't survive. A new report by the United Nations found that intimate partners or relatives kill an average of 137 women around the world each day.[4] This is a staggering number of murders of women.

> *Grace: The Kavanaugh hearing was very difficult to watch. His twisted mouth, frowning face, and uptight attitude were too much to bear. In this case, there was victim blaming—that Blasey Ford couldn't remember the story well, that her details were inconsistent, that she "was there" and so bears some of the responsibility. This narrative happens too often, and it was killing me on the*

inside. I could not imagine what it was doing to Blasey Ford as she was displayed on national television for everyone to see and to critique. Victims feel fear while the sexual violence is being committed, and that fear stays with them long after the abuse. Victims who overcome fear and share their stories of sexual violence are incredibly courageous and strong, and all I could think about during the Kavanaugh hearing was how courageous Blasey Ford was to step forward to share her story on a national stage. We need to hear victims' stories and accept their stories as truth rather than blaming them, which only instills deeper pain and suffering. We should not excuse or protect perpetrators—they have no excuse for their abusive actions.

Sexual Violence Is Not Just a Few Bad Acts

Addressing sexual violence has always been central to women and gender studies. Surely the time has come—in fact, it is long overdue—for it to be central for the church. The church cannot continue to sweep sexual violence under the rug and pretend it is not happening in the church, in the youth director's office, in the homes of parishioners, in the pastor's car, and just about everywhere both inside and outside the church walls. The church must acknowledge the reality of sexual violence and deal with it honestly to offer healing to survivors and to prevent future abuse.

Shannon: I grew up in the Lutheran church, but my mom was Catholic and felt guilty about my sister and me being Lutheran, so I often felt like both. My abuser was my father, who was the one who insisted we be Lutheran like his family. He was an alcoholic, was verbally and emotionally abusive, and started raping me when I was five. My parents dropped us off at Sunday school every week and went out to breakfast so we received mixed messages about the value of church and faith. (Not to mention the disparity between insisting we go to Sunday school but also being so horribly abusive.) My main issue with my church is that they had to know that we were living in an abusive setting—this was extreme abuse of all kinds throughout the family—and they preached love but did nothing to help us.

Even when the church has acknowledged abuse, it has usually framed it as the bad acts of a few individuals. Rarely has the church delved into the larger and more difficult questions which underlie abuse—gender and power. Sexual abuse is not about the proverbial few bad apples; rather it is a central feature of our society. Understanding how gender and power are at work in sexual abuse is an essential step toward imagining how to resist and prevent abuse, transform abusive culture, and love and support survivors.

Gender is a complicated identity. However, the dominant US culture (which is patriarchal) sees gender as binary, based on biology: male and female. This binary is a *hierarchy*, in which men, and the traits associated with them (strength, dominance, superiority, "rationality"), are valued *over* women and the traits associated with them (weakness, submission, inferiority, "emotionality"). Patriarchy gives more power to men, in all areas of society, including family, social, economic, political, and religious arenas. It is worth emphasizing that patriarchy, *not* God or nature, creates this hierarchy—and then spends enormous energy within all of these institutions to keep that power in place.

Sexual violence is a form of gender-based violence. Gender-based violence happens when people assert power over others based on gender. But it is not simply the result of unequal power between two people, but of people acting within this *system* of male dominance. Crucially, this system of seeing things as opposites (male/female, white/Black, straight/gay, etc.) and then *ranking* one above the other means that any person or group who is seen as feminine or feminized in some way (by being weak, poor, queer, etc.) is a target for violence. Therefore, gender-based violence includes men's violence against women, sexual abuse of children, violence against LGBTQ people, and sexualized violence against other men. All these forms of gender-based violence must be acknowledged if we want to move toward a nonviolent world.

Susan: One night when I was in seminary (I was about twenty-two years old), my best friend and I had gone to a movie at the dollar cinema just up the road from the campus. As we were leaving after the show, a big crowd of people were milling around waiting for the next movie to start. As we made our way through the crowd, we passed a line of teenage boys who were being loud and obnoxious as they jostled along. As one of the boys and I walked past each other, he suddenly reached out and grabbed my breast and then walked on past like nothing had happened. I kept walking too, stunned. "Did that really just happen?" I wondered. Then I became furious. What in the hell made this teenage boy think he could do that? Here I was, simply walking along a sidewalk when I was sexually violated in public, in a crowd. This is how vulnerable women are. While most sexual assaults are perpetrated in private by someone we know, we also know that public spaces aren't safe for us either.

Sexual violence includes a broad range of behaviors, both nonphysical (like making obscene gestures, sending unwanted emails or inappropriate social media postings, making suggestive sexual comments, using sexist language, telling dirty jokes, and commenting about women's bodies) and physical (anything from standing too close or brushing against someone, to acts of unwanted touching, grabbing, or fondling; pressuring, coercing, or threatening someone for sex; stalking; sexual abuse; physical assault; and rape). All of these may also occur in queer-bashing, domestic violence, sex trafficking, and war crimes. In one way or another, these behaviors harm people by dehumanizing them and opening the way to discrimination, abuse, and violence.

> *Janet: I was twenty-four when I was targeted by an older colleague in my clinic workplace. When I expressed interest in his medical feedback machine, he invited me into his office for a demonstration, locking the door. As I sat, he knelt in front of me, running his hand up under my skirt, and saying, "Now don't be confused, because this means exactly what you think it means." I escaped by leaping up and running into the office manager's space.*
>
> *After a couple of weeks of having nightmares and trying to avoid him, I confided in the office manager, who went to the two clinic partners telling what he had done to me—and to her. The female partner believed us; the male partner brushed it off. But after they consulted a lawyer, who advised them that I could sue, the male partner took it seriously! They had a meeting with the perpetrator where he insisted they sign a "nondisclosure agreement"—and he moved into a new office building the next day. I learned later he'd been doing the same thing to other young women for years.*

Sexual violence is frequent in the United States and around the world. Men commit most sexual assaults and harassment. Survivors of sexual assault almost always know the perpetrators. Women with disabilities are especially vulnerable to sexual assault, as are men who are part of socially marginalized groups, such as gay, bisexual, and transgender men. And men frequently target transgender women, particularly trans women of color, for gender-based violence.[5]

Koreans use the word *han* to describe the enormous painful "unjust suffering" that comes from unresolved injustice like that in sexism and racism. *Han* is the piercing of the heart, which breaks it into tiny pieces and leaves the victim with enormous aching pain, which can be both physical and psychological. For example, Koreans who were colonized by Japan and invaded by countries like China have experienced enormous pain and terrible "unjust suffering," which causes *han*. This *han* gets carried in our bodies and can be carried or passed through several generations. The burden and pain of *han* must be released if any healing is to occur. Many Christians turn to Christ to help them release their *han*, which in turn will bring some sense of wholeness and healing. Gender-based violence causes *han* to the victims, and survivors need to find ways to release *han* from ourselves. Otherwise, *han* will eat away at our bodies, souls, and lives.

Grace: When I was growing up, I often heard this Korean phrase: "han-mae-chi-da." It is a commonly uttered phrase by Korean women who have suffered intense pain from abusive husbands or from others who cause immense suffering and han. They would sit on the floor and pound their chest with their clasped fists and moan the phrase han-mae-chi-da *as they experience heartbreak, loss, pain, and destruction. This phrase* han-mae-chi-da *basically means that one is extremely overcome with han to the point that one becomes paralyzed and is in a state of severe sorrow, distress, and grief. Many women cried out the phrase* han-mae-chi-da *as a form of lament to wail and release their sorrow.*

When I was going through abuse, this is exactly how I felt. My body and spirit were in a state of being filled with han-mae-chi-da. *I was facing what the older Korean women are articulating every time they suffered from abuse, injustice, and intense torment. My entire body, mind, and spirit became paralyzed by* han *as I wallowed in hopelessness, pain, and despair. I became immobile and frozen in the depths of my suffering and pain. I felt like an utterly useless human being who was nonfunctioning due to scars and pain in my body.*

Sexual Violence Intersects with Gender, Race, Nationality, Sexual Identity, and Class

People often treat sexual abuse as a problem of individuals—a bad priest, a pedophile coach, or a drunken husband. However, in women and gender studies we recognize that sexual violence overlaps and combines with other factors such as gender, race/ethnicity, class, national origin, age, physical or mental ability, and sexual identity. We use the term "intersection" to describe these interactions. People in less valued groups (seen as "inferior" in the hierarchy) are affected much more often than people in highly valued groups (those who are seen as "superior" in the hierarchy). Within this system, sexual violence happens so often as to seem "normal." The following examples show some of the ways gender intersects with other forms of difference in violence. These are also examples of hate crimes, crimes that target people based on race, nationality, sexuality, gender identity, ability, or age. In addition to harming the victims of the crime, hate crimes also terrorize other members of the targeted group(s). The message is clear, that any member of the group could have been the person targeted.

In each of these examples we might ask, "Where is God? How could God let these things happen? What kind of God allows these atrocities?" More productive questions, however, might be, "What unequal structures of power allow sexual violence to persist? Whose purpose is served by the pervasiveness of sexual violence? Why do we as a society not effectively confront sexual violence?" These examples let us see how in our culture sexual violence is both normalized—expected as inevitable—and invisible when we ignore the ways that gender is at work in all kinds of violence. In the church, we often hear of these instances as manifestations of sinfulness and the acts of individual sinful people. Too often, we hear blame for victims, as if they somehow invited their violation. We hear responses of "thoughts and prayers," which often leave survivors feeling unseen, unbelieved, and unsupported. Thoughts and prayers don't change the dynamics of gender or the social systems that continue to allow sexual violence.

These examples demonstrate the setup for abuse that is part and parcel of patriarchal society. Men, especially straight white men, learn messages about what it means to be a man, what is owed men, and how men should act. One of the clear messages of patriarchal masculinity is that to be a man is to exert power-over, and we see in these instances how power-over gets expressed as sexual violence. Another significant piece of the setup for abuse is the way the church often teaches us to accept sexual violence as the will of God. By telling us that God is in control of everything, the church leads us to believe that God must send sexual violence—to test us or to punish us—and so we learn to accept sexual violence as part of the divine plan.

These atrocities, however, help us see the flaw in such thinking. We see that sexual violence is not from God but is a choice made by humans within patriarchal systems that perpetuate sexual violence. And we see that when the church teaches sexual violence is somehow within the will of God, the church is also participating in the violence. Throughout this book, we want to turn traditional Christian thinking about sexual violence on its head. Instead of starting with God or the Bible or Christian belief, we start with survivors' experiences and the honest and hard questions that come from experiencing sexual violence. As you read these examples, think about the questions they raise from victims' perspectives. What might we learn about God if we start with these victims' experiences?

Mass Shootings. We might not automatically think about mass shootings as sexual violence, but when we look deeper we see that the links are there. Mass shooters have one thing in common: almost all of them are men.[6] Many men, especially young men, turn to mass shooting to demonstrate or defend their masculinity. Most have a history of misogyny (woman-hating) and violence against women; some specifically target women. Some of the killers are "incels" ("involuntary celibates"), misogynistic men who believe women owe them sex and who are enraged at women for "denying" them this. They have seized on the dark web ("the manosphere"), to spew their hatred of women and find camaraderie with other spurned men.

One incel "hero," Elliot Rodger, killed six people (women, and men of color) in 2014, after posting a video to YouTube, lamenting his virginity and detailing his plan for a "Day of Retribution." He targeted a sorority with "the kind of girls I've always desired but was never able to have."[7]

In 2021 a young white man attacked three Atlanta-area spas, carefully targeted because they were staffed by Asian and Asian American women. A witness claimed the young man shouted, "Kill all Asians," as he carried out his rampage. In spite of the fact that he claimed he was motivated by a sex addiction (which he blamed on the spas), not racial bias, it is apparent that race and gender were inseparable in this crime.

Grace: I have always felt that Asian American women were hypersexualized in North American society. This is in part due to historical stereotyping of Asian American women as sex workers, such as the character in the popular opera Madame Butterfly. *Many Asian women who immigrated in the late 1800s and early 1900s were single and were trafficked or lured into prostitution. Thus, there was an early understanding and view of Asian women as sexualized bodies. This understanding has carried on to our present context where Asian American women are viewed as sexual objects who exist to please and pleasure men.*

In certain ways, I often feel objectified by men who see me and other Asian American women as hypersexualized bodies. It affects me as I walk down the street, ride subway trains, and sit in cafes to drink and eat. I always need to be aware of the surroundings and be cautious as men see my gender and my race and already have misperceptions, and misportrayals of who I am. I often tell my young college-age daughter to always be careful of her surroundings as she walks around on campus. Due to this hypersexualization of Asian American women, atrocities happen like the Atlanta spa killings and also sexually violent raping and killing of young Asian American women on university campuses.

In both murder cases mentioned above, the killers expressed stereotypical views of the women they focused on (highly sexualized images of sorority women and Asian women, who failed to please the shooters as they felt entitled to). It is apparent that these stereotypes were on the men's minds as they murdered the women they targeted.

Police Killings of Black People. People may look at the problem of police killing Black people as mostly an issue of race, but it is also an issue of class and gender that frequently includes sexual violence. Legal scholar Kimberlé Crenshaw started the Say Her Name project to highlight the scope of police violence against Black and other women of color and Black transgender and gender nonbinary people, especially those living in poverty.[8] Evidence from the project shows that police project stereotypes onto their interactions with Black women (such as that they are likely to be drug mules), that police are less likely to protect Black women in violent situations such as domestic violence, and that they may actually *target* women of color for violence, including sexual harassment and sexual assault. Further, much of this violence is ignored or minimized: Consider the case of Breonna Taylor, a Black woman killed by Louisville police as she lay unarmed, in her own bed. The only convictions made were for officers firing blindly into another apartment, not for killing Breonna Taylor. Womanist (Black feminist) theologian Kelly Brown Douglas says the problem is the stereotype of the hypersexualized Black body.[9] This stereotype depicts Black women as temptresses and Black men as predators. Douglas argues that this stereotype was essential to justify enslaving Black people and sexually exploiting their bodies through forced breeding and rape. If Black bodies are hypersexualized, they are also intrinsically sinful and guilty and a threat to the white supremacist social order. This belief means that police perceptions of Black people begin in assumptions of guilt and danger that justify violence, including sexual violence, against Black people.

Murders of Indigenous Women. In 2021, Secretary of the Interior Deb Haaland created a unit within the Bureau of Indian Affairs to address the crisis of missing and murdered Indigenous women in the United States. For decades, thousands of Indigenous girls and women have disappeared or been killed, their cases going unsolved, often ignored by law enforcement. Murder rates for Indigenous women are ten times the national average. (Many other countries see similar rates of violence against Indigenous women as well.) While Black women's experiences of gender-based violence in the United States are shaped by the legacy of the enslavement of Africans, Indigenous women's experiences are shaped by the legacy of settler colonialism (a system when an invader group defeats and displaces Indigenous groups, taking their land and resources through violent processes of killing, removal, subjugation, and erasure. Dominant cultures impose hierarchical structures that maintain dominance using institutions such as government, education, healthcare, and religion). This system treats Indigenous women's bodies as sites for conquest and control. For example, the federal government denied tribes the right to prosecute crimes by nontribal members (usually white men) committed on their land until a Supreme Court decision in 2015 finally allowed tribes to prosecute nontribal members— but only if the victim has an established relationship with the perpetrator! That means a non-Indigenous stranger who rapes a woman or abuses a child on tribal land cannot be prosecuted by the tribe. Prosecution is left to the federal government, which seldom follows up on these cases.

Murders of BIPOC Trans Women. Black, Indigenous, and people of color (BIPOC) transgender women are similarly at risk for sexual assault and murder, and governments are often not interested in investigating the crimes. The years 2020 and 2021 were two of the deadliest ever for murders of transgender people in the United States, with the majority of those murdered being BIPOC, and the majority of those being women. Leaders of the religious/political Right in the United States have turned their attention to transgender people: anti-trans bills would limit trans youth's access to medical assistance in transitioning and prevent trans girls and women from participating in women's sports. Religious groups, like Southern Baptists, have published statements condemning transgender identities as incompatible with God's will. By heightening anti-trans rhetoric, these actions contribute to a climate of hostility toward trans people, increase the risk of anti-trans violence, including sexual violence, and take an emotional toll on trans people, who are traumatized by these attacks on their very being.

Sexual Assaults during Border Crossings. Around 80 percent of women and girls who try to cross the border between the United States and Mexico experience sexual violence—from fellow migrants, people smugglers, government officials, and border police. Many women are forced to exchange sex for passage because they do not have the money to pay people smugglers (to the point that many women start taking birth control before their border crossing). They may also be forced into sex work, beaten, and even killed. Survivors often hesitate to come forward, ashamed for having been raped, afraid reporting might derail their attempt to cross the border, or afraid they might be subjected to further sexual violence by authorities. Ironically, many of these women are trying to escape gender-based violence in their own countries. Yet seeking asylum in the United States is notoriously difficult, and, as many of them wait to have their cases heard, they must work in low wage jobs, in insecure financial situations that continue and perhaps even increase their vulnerability to gender-based violence.

Genocide and Rape in Guatemala. From 1960 to 1996, Guatemala's government targeted Indigenous Mayans for defending their land, water, and cultural rights. The government wiped out villages, killed or "disappeared" thousands of people, and tortured many. Women were especially targeted for rape and sexual slavery, often being forced to cook and clean for the soldiers who raped them as a weapon of war. This tore the very fabric of Mayan society. Despite the fact that the armed conflict ended, and that a few military officers were tried for these crimes, Guatemalan women still face high rates of poverty, illiteracy, racial discrimination, and one of the highest rates of femicide (murders of females) in the world.

During this, the evangelical church in Guatemala grew under the nation's first evangelical president, Efraín Ríos Montt, supported by US president Ronald Reagan and American evangelical missionaries, who helped as Ríos Montt's representatives among the Maya. Ríos Montt was later convicted of genocide and crimes against humanity.

Many Mayan women who were violated during the genocide have used Indigenous spiritual practices to move toward healing. Ceremonies, rituals, weaving, and theater are just a few of the ways many Mayan women have reclaimed ancient spiritual practices to help them heal from the trauma of a genocidal war. Many of these women have also turned to the courts to seek justice, and in 2022 five paramilitary fighters were sentenced to prison for their rapes of Maya Achi women during the internal armed conflict.

Worldwide Legislation Against LGBTQ People. In 2021, LGBTQ people faced unprecedented attacks through legislation. In the United States, a historic number of anti-LGBTQ bills were introduced, with many becoming law. These included preventing trans girls and women from participating in women's sports, preventing teachers from even mentioning LGBTQ issues, and giving service providers such as healthcare workers the right to refuse service to someone based on their perceived gender or sexual identity. In Poland, nearly one hundred cities have signed anti-"LGBT ideology" resolutions or "family charters" that support only married heterosexual couples. As major churches across Africa oppose LGBTQ rights, governments such as those in Senegal, Nigeria, and Ghana are turning to laws that severely penalize LGBTQ people. The situation was worsened by the COVID-19 pandemic, which led some to scapegoat LGBTQ people, blaming them for outbreaks, or sweeping them up in arrests on the pretense they were breaking Covid restrictions. Whenever anti-LGBTQ propaganda and legislation increase, violence, including sexual violence, against LGBTQ people also increases, and worldwide we are seeing just such a surge in anti-LGBTQ violence.

Susan: With the Supreme Court's overturn of Roe v. Wade, *the decision that affirmed the right to choose abortion as a constitutional right, many pundits believe the Christian Right will soon attempt to overturn marriage equality as a constitutional right as well. In fact, a number of Christian Right leaders and politicians have explicitly stated this goal. Now I worry that my marriage could be compromised. Marriage bestows a wide range of rights and privileges—from making healthcare decisions to inheritance to health insurance. More importantly, it offers a social affirmation of a relationship that plays an important role in helping relationships stay healthy and lasting. To imagine that the Supreme Court may take away marriage as a fundamental right for queer people feels like a violation of my very personhood. I wonder if straight people can even begin to imagine what this must feel like. While President Biden signed the Respect for Marriage Act in December 2022, its protections are limited. States may have to recognize my marriage, but, if Obergefell is overturned, states will be able to decide whether or not to allow same-sex marriages. In 2023, the Supreme Court decided businesses can deny services to LGBTQ people based on owners' and workers' religious convictions. I wonder how the Christian Right can embrace a God they believe would be so cruel as they are.*

These examples demonstrate how gender, race/ethnicity, social class, and sexuality intersect within sexual violence and how religion plays a role in normalizing, perpetuating, and even approving sexual violence. In this book, we focus on sexual violence and its impact on how we think about God, the Bible, and Christian faith. Survivors will have different experiences and different ways of coping with abuse, but most will face painful questions of why and how such experiences were allowed to happen to them.

Susan: Experiencing childhood sexual abuse led me to reject the idea of an all-powerful, controlling God who either willed or allowed my abuse; this sent me on a theological quest to reconcile my experiences of abuse with my understanding of God as love.

Grace: It has been a lifelong theological journey to move away from a patriarchal notion of God which seemed to perpetuate dominance and subjugation of women. This dominance includes sexual violence, sexual slavery, and sexual manipulation, all committed in the name of God and Christianity.

The masculine, all-powerful, almighty image of God continues to sanction physical, verbal, and sexual abuse toward the vulnerable, powerless, and marginalized in society, but this remains unspoken on the whole in Christian communities. Sexual abuse helps shore up patriarchy and men's dominance over women. So, it is usually swept under the rug and even normalized in Christian families, communities, and churches. For the church to move away from ignoring and accepting sexual violence, churches must move away from a dominating patriarchal notion of a God who must be obeyed without ques tion and toward a more liberative understanding of a God who loves, welcomes, and embraces all people.

CHAPTER 2

Surviving God

Laura: I thought God loved me, but I didn't understand why He never answered my prayers to be rescued. I remember imagining Him turning to look away while the abuse was happening, kind of like He did while Jesus was on the cross.

Susan: During the years of my abuse, I thought of God as a stern and disapproving authority figure. God's love for me wasn't conditional, but God's approval and blessing were. I had always taken the messages of the church seriously. I walked the aisle and made my profession of faith when I was only six years old during a revival with a hellfire-and-damnation traveling evangelist whose sermons gave me nightmares about waking up in hell. So a few years later when my abuse started, it wasn't a big leap for me to take responsibility for my "choice" to let myself be abused. After all, at six I had already understood myself as wicked enough to deserve hell. Why wouldn't I be responsible because I didn't stop what was happening to me? My prayers weren't for God to make it stop but for God to give me the strength to make it stop. This was a test for me in God's permissible will, and I was failing it miserably.

Grace: The only God that I was introduced to was a white male God. A white male God was a stern, powerful, almighty, and conqueror God. This God was a patriarchal God who preferred men over women. In a patriarchal world, women were made subordinate and were dominated by men, which included sexual domination, sexual abuse, and mental abuse. In my patriarchal world, culture, and family, a white male God gave legitimacy to the abuse that I was experiencing. It was almost a given that something like this would happen to me, and there was nothing that I could do to prevent it or stop it. A white male God almost gives permission to men to abuse me and prevent me from speaking out about it.

What Kind of God?

"What kind of God?" We imagine many survivors have asked this question. What kind of God allows children to be abused? What kind of God lets pastors prey on teenagers in their congregations? What kind of God tells women and children to submit to fathers who hit and abuse them? What kind of God tells armies to destroy entire nations and take the women as a prize? For survivors of sexual violence, none of these images make any sense. Rather, they increase our pain and confusion.

Too often the church answers our questions with images that only reinforce harm. "God has a plan," they say. "Who are we to question God's wisdom?" "Stay with your husband," pastors may advise, "and God will change him." "You have to forgive your abuser because the Bible tells us to forgive." "God's ways are not our ways." We even sang, "Farther along, we'll know all about it. Farther along, we'll understand why." God has a divine plan, many a church leader intoned, and whatever happens to us is part of the plan, and we should rejoice in it.

For survivors, these answers hardly alleviate the suffering and shame that come with abuse. In fact, the God of these answers comes to look very much like our abusers, gaslighting us with the idea that abuse is love, and silence is faithfulness.

Asian Americans, for example, live in a culture of "honor/shame" in which abuse is shameful; opening up and sharing about abuse is very difficult for victims of sexual violence. Many continue to stay and live silently with their abusive husbands because of the shame and fear that they themselves may be blamed. Many abused Asian American women would rather live with abuse and potential death by murder than live with the shame of people knowing they have an abusive husband. The shame will not just fall on them and their husbands but also on their children, their parents, and the entire extended family.

The God many Christians imagine is an overlord moving people and nature around in some preordained play. No matter what the violation, all is well because it is God's will. The abuse is all part of God's divine plan, and, therefore, it should not be a problem for survivors. These images of God, however, are often devastating to survivors because they make God an accomplice in, if not directly responsible for, their abuse and their suffering. They make it very hard for survivors to heal, to understand what happened to them, and to relate to God. Some leave Christianity because they cannot reconcile the contradictions, pain, and suffering with their understanding of God.

One survivor who wrote poetry to help her process her trauma puts it this way:

She Questions Her Poetry

Is it a lie
to write these words—
to spit angry images
in the face of God
to scar the horizontal landscape
with curving female figures
to bleed my pain
on the uncomfortable bed?

Is it hypocrisy
to speak my word
in the language of metaphor
against deaf ears?

It is hypocrisy
to speak

in times like these
when silence is secure?

I cannot close my eyes
but I see a crucifix
where broken body
still hangs
always hangs

(there is fear here
in this spoken word
real as bare feet
on broken glass)

Is it a lie
because the torn dress
and bloody thighs
often make this
cross of gold
hang heavy
around my neck?

Grace: As a survivor of sexual abuse, it was most difficult to share any of my abuse with anyone. Due to shame, I could not talk to other family members, friends, or anyone outside of my community. If others knew about my experiences of abuse, no one would want to associate with me or my family. Therefore, I had this huge shameful burden to carry with me. I had to pretend that everything was all right when nothing was. It was much later as an adult that I was able to open up about my experience of abuse to my pastor and to a counselor. This took me enormous willpower to overcome the shame that would befall me in order to seek help.

Images of God

Our images of God matter. When we speak of God, we are trying to express the Infinite in finite language, and so, of course, our language about God is always incomplete and inadequate. Metaphors and analogies to talk about God are necessary to give our minds some way to try to imagine the incomprehensible. We cannot do without metaphors[1] because they are an essential part of the human need to make meaning, and they help us make sense of the Divine. Metaphors help us understand difficult concepts by comparing something hard to grasp to something familiar, for example, by saying God is a father. A good metaphor moves us to see our familiar world in a new light.[2]

Metaphors always reflect the cultures that produce them. They carry the assumptions, preferences, and biases of a culture and can maintain systems of power. So, for example, thinking of God as a king can reinforce the political system of monarchy. If God the King deserves our allegiance, so might an earthly king. The image of king validates colonialism: the usurping of other people's land and resources, in the process often slaughtering them and/or erasing their cultures, languages, and identities. It also evokes the image of empire and empire building, where subjects are under the power of the ruler. An example is the westward expansion across North America of white European settlers in the nineteenth century, many of them believing they were bringing "civilization" to "savage" peoples, driven by the conviction that their actions were part of a "manifest destiny," that it was God's will for them to dominate the continent. We have seen other such consequences, as white Christians colonized the Americas, Africa, and Asia.

As another example, if we think of God as white, then we may well imagine white people as somehow more like God than Black, Indigenous, and people of color. Throughout church history, white European men upheld God in their own image and have used that image to justify the domination of BIPOC around the world. In the United States, the whiteness of God is a cornerstone of white supremacy, from genocide against Indigenous peoples to the enslavement of Africans, racial segregation, the use of indentured Asian workers, and modern practices of incarceration and anti-immigration. White supremacy has justified xenophobia, Islamophobia, anti-Semitism, and hatred toward BIPOC and immigrants. For example, during the coronavirus pandemic, the United States experienced a sharp rise in hate crimes against Asian Americans, with murders throughout the country. The ongoing portrayal of God as white supports white people's discriminatory actions toward people of color.

These images of God can easily become fixed over time, so that we assume they are eternal rather than reflections of a particular culture, time, or place. We begin to think of them as actual portrayals of God, and we accept the associations that come with these images as God's will. Philosopher Alfred North Whitehead called this way of thinking the "fallacy of misplaced concreteness."[3] By that, he meant that people turn abstract ideas into concrete realities. So, if we only use male images of God, we begin to think of God as male. If we think of God as male, we can accept patriarchy as a God-ordained system. If we think of God as Master, we may think of slavery as an institution of God's will.

What we relate to, then, is an image of God, not God. When we accept these images as actual, concrete, or literal, we make them idolatrous. These are the graven images that are warned against in the Ten Commandments (Exodus 20:1–17).

To avoid substituting the image for the reality, we must constantly challenge harmful images of God. We must evaluate our own images of God to see if they are just and liberative. We must also recognize that the images we hold can be helpful and limiting at the same time. For example, if we think of God as Father, we may miss all the ways God participates in nurturing activities. That's because, within patriarchy, we think of fathers as strong; they provide for the family; they protect; they make rules and enforce them. We think of activities like caring for children, nursing sick people, and providing for daily bodily needs as mothering, and women's work. Because within patriarchy we see women as gentle, meek, and caring, we gender nurturing work as female. If our images of God only make room for male images, such as Father, we ignore or minimize God's work in healing, nurturing, and caring, and we limit the ways we may feel God working in mothering ways in our lives.

It's especially important to challenge images that are used in any way to marginalize, harm, or oppress people. We have seen that people in power often cast God in their own images and then use those images to justify mistreatment of people who are not like them. Some people may even identify so strongly with those images that they believe they are channeling God or that they *are* God. We must be aware of the ways images of God can be used for harm and reject those images.

During the storming of the US Capitol on January 6, 2021, rioters carried crosses and signs reading "Jesus Saves" and "Jesus 2020." They chanted, "Christ is King," and referred to the Proud Boys (an exclusively male organization of far-right neofascists) as "God's warriors." Many of them believed that Donald Trump was specially anointed by God to save Christians from persecution in the wider society—some even believed that their riot was a holy crusade, commanded by God. Many of the rioters were white Christian nationalists, who believe the United States is supposed to be a Christian rather than a secular nation. This form of white supremacy seeks to install white Christian men as lawmakers and decision-makers for all people. It is rooted in the image of a white God who only loves and prefers white people. As January 6th and other Christian nationalist actions have shown, a white male image of God feeds Christian nationalism, white supremacy, and white patriarchy. These are all dangerous as they contribute to discrimination and hatred and justify white violence against people of color and all women.

Rather than holding onto specific images as uniquely representative of God, we should use what we have called "kaleidoscopic" imagery.[4] By this we mean that we should hold multiple shifting images of God all at once rather than the single notion of a white male God, which has led to so much violence. Since no single image can reflect all of who God is, we need many to help us recognize the multiple aspects of God's presence in the world. We need these images to be in motion so we don't get stuck on any one image, or think we've somehow completely grasped who God is. We need to create new images of God which are liberative, loving, and welcoming. As cultures and attitudes change, we need new images that are relevant to the moment and challenge us to think of God differently in different contexts.

For example, ecofeminist theologian Sallie McFague encouraged us to create new models of God to challenge the patriarchal images which were destructive to humanity and also to God's creation.[5] She suggested God as mother, lover, and companion and the earth as God's body. New models, she explained, should surprise and shock us because they reveal something we haven't really thought about yet. These images can help us dismantle sexism, racism, and climate injustice.

Susan: For me, the new model for God that helped most was God as the quantum energy of the universe. Yes, I know that's a little heady, but that's just me. I found this image in process theology, and it resonated. This image draws on the field of quantum physics—which is mostly way above my head, but, thankfully, I was able to take a seminar with John Cobb, one of the originators of process theology. In the image of God as the quantum energy of the universe, God is the cosmic energy, the creative lifeforce, of every quantum (the smallest possible particle of everything), in every particle, experiencing every particle, calling every particle to fulfill its divine intention. This is complex, but stay with me because this revelation saved me. The God of process thinking is not controlling or coercive but is present in and affected by what happens to every particle. What that meant for me as a survivor was clear—God did not cause or control my abuse, but God suffered with me in it.

New metaphors can expand and reimagine our traditional language, understanding, and imagination about God. So, for example, thinking of God as Black may serve as both a comforting image for BIPOC and a disruptive image for white people, who may be challenged to see how they have unconsciously held an image of God as white and how this image has affected the treatment of people of color in society. We need new images today which can challenge the structures that uphold sexual violence, particularly among Christians.

Grace: New metaphors can shift our patterns of habitual thinking and thrust us to new ways of thinking about old images which may cause initial discomfort to our faith and understanding. This applies to our concept and understanding of God. God as a woman, mother, and grandmother shifts the power dynamics and gives room to grow as a woman. In Korean culture, mothers and grandmothers nurture, develop, and grow a family. Mothers and grandmothers are essential to the family, as it is they who teach, nurture, guide, and form the child. In many ways, mothers and grandmothers do everything they can to protect their children from harm, abuse, and destruction. This image is beautiful to me as it opens the door to a nurturing God who wants the best for us. I don't have to be fearful of an almighty, angry God, but rather can embrace a Mothering God who gives us life and protects us from harm. As a survivor, I know God was and is always with me as a loving mother and a grandmother who protects their young.

Intersectionality and God

Looking at our images of God through an intersectional lens is an important way to ensure our images are kaleidoscopic, reflect a broad variety of human experience, and move our images toward justice. An intersectional lens helps us keep in mind all the ways that social differences—gender, race/ethnicity, class, sexuality, ability, age, education, nation, and religion—are at work, shaping our images and understandings of God. Intersectionality also reminds us to make our thinking "both-and" rather than "either/or." "Both-and" thinking lets us hold in mind multiple, sometimes even competing, images that reflect our experiences and the experiences of others. So, for example, biblical images of God as Wisdom (Greek *Sophia*) and Reason (*logos*) remind us that images of God can be feminine as well as masculine.

Aspects of race and ethnicity can also enrich images of God. Mercy Amba Oduyoye imagines God as "Householder" from the perspective of African women's experience.[6] For many families in Africa, women are still the primary caregivers in the home. God the Householder is a mother who helps and cares for Her family. God the Householder can comfort victims of sexual violence in their turmoil, pain, and anguish.

The dominant images and words about God we have inherited promote misogyny, racial hierarchies, colonialism, homophobia and transphobia, child abuse, and sexual violence. We need to search out images, words, and language that can enlarge our incomplete pictures of God, especially ones that nurture us, spark the creative in us, and celebrate the glorious diversity among us. Intersectional thinking can help nudge us away from the binary thinking of male/female, white/Black, et cetera, and in the direction of justice. As one survivor said, "We have to unlearn ideas of God that don't work anymore."

Most of us learned images of God as all-powerful, domi-nant, unmoved, and unmoving. This kind of God aligns much better with the power of dominators, colonizers, enforcers, and abusers. Behind this image is a fear of weakness and vulnerability which are identified with femininity and women. The image of an all-powerful God is a reflection of patriarchal devotion to power, especially power over women and other marginalized people. This is not an image that is especially comforting or helpful to many survivors who have experienced powerlessness, helplessness, and weakness. We know what it is to be at the mercy of those with power over us, and this image makes God one more relationship with controlling power over our lives. This image justifies power-over and suggests that to be like God is to exercise power-over. Intersectional thinking helps us identify how this image then perpetuates patriarchy, imperialism, wealth inequality, racism, and other oppressions as it constructs God on the side of dominating power.

Intersectional thinking also offers alternatives to the all-powerful God who dominates and conquers. For example, when we draw from the stories of diverse survivors, those who by definition have been powerless and dominated, we can begin to imagine God as vulnerable. This God is no stoic. Rather this God is affected by everything that happens in the universe. This God feels pain and suffering as well as joy and contentment. This vulnerable God takes into God's own experience of being every feeling, every emotion, every longing, every success, and every failure of each and every particle of the universe. God feels the universe and is deeply affected by it. In other words, God's vulnerability means God experiences what we experience and feels what we feel. God knows our pain because God experiences it with us, and, in experiencing it with us, God survives with us and calls us in love to survive and thrive. This vulnerable God looks like a Ukrainian widow in war-torn Mariupol, a young mother and her children on their first night in a domestic violence shelter, a pregnant ten-year-old denied an abortion by lawmakers, a brutally beaten gay South African man, a Catholic altar boy molested by his priest, and a Southern Baptist teenager sexually assaulted by her youth pastor.

An intersectional lens also helps us understand the impacts of various images of God. An image that is comforting to some people may be traumatizing for others. The image of God as the male head of the household may feel threatening and disturbing to women and children who experience domestic violence. Or the image of God as judge may be traumatizing to a rape survivor who has been failed by the justice system. In fact, a great deal of modern theology maintains sexual violence by presenting a male God who demands women and children submit to men, condemns LGBTQ people, and sends warriors to defeat dehumanized foreign enemies.

Finally, an intersectional lens helps us see that our thinking about God isn't clear-cut but sometimes messy and unclear. The church has preached a very clear-cut theology and understanding of God that maintains the church's status quo, which in turn has helped maintain heterosexual white male dominance. The church has preached a simplistic message of who God is for all people, as though any one group can articulate the fullness of God for everyone. Intersectional feminist and liberation thinking challenge the rigidity of traditional ways of thinking about God that claim to speak for everyone and express unchanging truths. These liberatory ways of thinking about God underline the messiness, multiplicity, and fluidity of people's relationships with the Divine.

Context matters, and each person brings something important from their own particular experiences and perspectives to the ways we see and understand God. Especially, when we listen to the voices of women across their differences, including survivors of sexual violence, we gain insights about God that are missing from traditional white male theology. These perspectives challenge traditional views of God that can limit, constrict, and oppress. Because many traditional images play a role in enabling sexual violence, challenging and even eliminating them is necessary work.

CHAPTER 3

Troubling Beliefs

Around the world, we've seen the church implicated in sexual violence. The Catholic Church prioritizes abusive priests over parishioners, and we are still learning the scope of abuse by priests and indifference by the church. In many war-torn places, churches have aligned themselves with authoritarian leaders who have encouraged violence, including rape as a tool of war. We've also seen religious communities cast out victims of rape, blaming them for the violence perpetrated against them. Southern Baptists, the nation's largest Protestant denomination, are in the midst of a reckoning for their indifference to survivors and enablement of abusive pastors and other church leaders. For Christians, sexual violence is often tied up with certain troubling beliefs and church practices that actually open the door for abuse and make it difficult for survivors to come forward and seek justice.

Forgiveness

Certain notions of salvation and forgiveness contribute to and uphold a culture of abuse. In some evangelical thinking, a person only needs to ask God for forgiveness to be forgiven—and although they should be genuinely sorry and intend never to commit a sin again, salvation and forgiveness do not require any kind of apology or reparation to the people they have wronged. Forgiveness from God is easy, and it almost grants a person a "pass" on whatever wrong they have committed. This easy form of forgiveness is what German theologian Dietrich Bonhoeffer calls "cheap grace."[1] It is a form of grace, or God's gift, that we bestow upon ourselves. Cheap grace is forgiveness without real repentance or grace without discipleship; it is grace without the cross. It is cheap because nothing is required of us. Bonhoeffer shares that a "costly grace" confronts us as a call to follow Jesus. To follow Jesus requires action, discipline, and care for one another. It requires us to act and become different. It pushes us to look at the person whom we have wronged and not only ask forgiveness but also make restitution and bring about transformation in the relationship. It reminds us that our faith isn't just about a vertical relationship with God, but it is equally about horizontal relationships with other people. The cheap grace that the church often teaches is that God forgives even if the perpetrator never makes anything right with the victim. The perpetrator does not even have to acknowledge the pain that they have caused the victim, as forgiveness comes from God and every sin will be "wiped away." Hence there is no need to linger in remorse about sin as God has forgiven the perpetrator. In this way of thinking, some Christians easily accept, for example, that, even if Brett Kavanaugh committed acts of sexual assault as a young man, if he asked God for forgiveness, all is forgiven—and there's no need for further action. Forgiveness is understood as "easy" forgiveness, an extension of "grace" which requires no reform, no soul-searching work, no transformation of those who commit sexual violence.

This kind of theological forgiveness means perpetrators can move on with no consequences and no concern for the people they victimized. According to many of Kavanaugh's defenders, because he seems to be a good man who has lived an upstanding life since his high school misdeeds, that is evidence enough that he is forgiven and has no need to account for, much less atone for, what he did—despite its ongoing effects on the life of

Christine Blasey Ford, and the other survivors who joined her in accusing him of assault and even rape.

> *Jo: I feel so lucky that I was so well educated and so drawn to liberation because I got out, but I'm saddened that I'm the only one in my family that has left, and all of us were sexually abused. I don't have evidence it was everyone, but I have a lot of cousins and a lot of them came forward when I did and they're like, "We just have to forgive. This is what God wants—the family to stay together." So, there is a strong theological narrative of manipulation. That is not God at all; that is not love at all. But it's certainly what my family teaches in order to keep women and children in the hands of violence—and that violence passing down through generations.*

In 1998, then-youth pastor Andy Savage drove a high school student home from church; along the way, he stopped and pressured her to give him oral sex. When she reported the incident, the pastor of the church allowed Savage to resign his youth minister position without public accountability—and so Savage moved on in his career with no real consequences. The incident only became public when his victim, motivated by newscaster Matt Lauer's 2017 removal from NBC, emailed Savage to ask if he remembered what he did. When Savage didn't respond, the woman went public. When Savage addressed the issue on a Sunday morning in front of his church, offering an apology to his victim and to the church, the congregation stood and applauded him.[2]

Christianity has been concerned for far too long about the vertical relationship between us and God. Christianity has focused on the sinner who has done something wrong against God rather than focusing on what we have done wrong against our neighbors. Christianity has oftentimes neglected to be troubled about the horizontal relationship between us and others, including the ways we sin against others. As a result,

Christianity has failed to focus on the "sinned against" or those whom we have wronged.

We need to try to make things right when we have wronged others. Korean theologians who do liberation theology have introduced the term *han*. The Korean word *han*, as discussed in chapter 1, reminds us that we need to be concerned about those who have been sinned against because of unjust actions within unjust systems in society like sexism, racism, and homophobia, which perpetuate harm, hurt, oppression, and discrimination and free perpetrators from accountability.

Han reminds us to focus on the other side of sin. *Han* is a terrible crushing feeling of the heart which a victim feels when a wrong is unresolved. If perpetrators only ask God to forgive, it frees them from the burden and responsibility to seek forgiveness from those they have directly hurt, damaged, wronged, and sinned against and to make restitution. If any healing is going to occur, we cannot forget the sinned against. We must remember the horizontal as well as the vertical relationship.

We know that nothing can ever erase abuse, and so the idea of making things right or restitution is complicated. When we think about this side of forgiveness, we must center the needs of the victim; the victim is the one who decides what restitution and making things as right as possible should look like because the point is to try to restore the victim's wholeness as much as can be done. This may mean, for example, the perpetrator needs to pay for the victim's counseling to deal with the abuse. Some victims may want a direct, face-to-face apology; some victims may never want to see their perpetrators again, and, if this is the case, the perpetrator is the one who needs to leave the spaces where the victim may be, whether a church or a home or a social setting. And, of course, if the perpetrator's behavior is criminal, it must be reported to the police, and the perpetrator should confess guilt and accept the consequences of the legal system. If the victim wants to restore some kind of relationship with the perpetrator, then the perpetrator must participate in the ways the victim requires, but the victim must also be free to end the relationship completely if that's what the victim needs. The church should be involved in these processes on the side of the victim, while also calling the perpetrator to full repentance and accountability. The possibility of redemption should remain open for the perpetrator, but the process should be clear that the victim is not the one responsible for bringing the perpetrator back into right relationship with God, the community, and the victim. Someone in the church should be involved in the process, but not the victim unless they want to be in some way.

This is all the other side of forgiveness which has, on the whole, been neglected in Christianity but needs to be brought back into our consciousness and everyday living. Too often Christianity has ignored the requirement to make things right again for survivors. Focusing only on the need for God's forgiveness and omitting the need for restitution and transformation has left survivors unaddressed and unsupported. We need to be mindful of the two sides of sin and both sides of forgiveness if perpetrators and survivors are to experience fully wholeness, holiness, and grace.

Laura: [My] sexual abuse [by my father] was accidentally exposed when a Girl Scout leader overheard a conversation between myself and another victim and insisted that I tell my mother. My mother called the police and had him arrested, then after the hearing changed her mind. She and my paternal grandmother hired a lawyer to brainwash and coach me for months on how to get him acquitted. My maternal grandparents were the "godly" influence in my life and aided in this endeavor so my parents could save the marriage, keep our family together, and keep my sister and I out of the foster system. Avoiding a family scandal was also ideal, as my maternal grandfather was a respected deacon in his church. After the acquittal, my atheist father made a show of crying out to

God on his knees and burning all the porn used in my grooming in the fireplace. There were declarations of returning to church and praying together as a family, which satisfied my maternal grandparents. The sexual abuse resumed within three months and continued until I rescued myself at the age of fifteen. I threatened to run away, so I was given a home with my "godly" grandparents who began using Scripture to silence me and train me to "minister to and love my dad" well so maybe God would use me to save him. The worst possible outcome was for me to refuse to forgive, become bitter, and ruin my life. So, for thirty-five years, I obeyed and continued to have relationship with both parents for the sake of the gospel. I got married, had three kids, and our life was all about God and being leaders in the church, until 2019 when I defended an abuse victim at my church. Our family was spiritually abused by leadership, and they defended the abuser. This rocked my world and began a deconstruction of all things spiritual.

In some parts of Christian culture, women are pressured to forgive their abusers, continuing a cycle in which men like Savage and Laura's father escape accountability. Once someone has repented and been forgiven by God, the thinking goes, no one should continue to hold something against him or make him accountable—and, in fact, the woman may herself be sinning by refusing to forgive.

Forgiveness, of course, means there's no need for restitution to the survivors, which explains why most of the concern we hear about men accused of abuse and assault is about *them*—the damage to their careers, the tarnishing of their reputations, the stress they must be feeling. Concerns about victims' suffering, the ongoing effects of abuse on their lives, and damages to their careers, reputations, families, and spirits are unimportant, because what happened is in the past and is erased by forgiveness. Perpetrators should be able to move on as if nothing happened. Victims should get over it. All is forgiven, washed clean in the blood of the Lamb.

Susan: I never confronted my abuser, but I did forgive him eventually, for me, not for him. For me forgiveness means I no longer wish someone harm. It doesn't mean I pretend nothing happened. I realized that there was nothing my abuser could ever say that would satisfy me. I didn't want to hear him say, "I'm sorry." It wouldn't have made any difference. And I certainly didn't want to feel pressure to say, "It's ok." It's not ok. It will never be ok. I will always carry the scars of abuse with me. And there was nothing he could do or say that could have made anything better. I forgave him because it helped me let go of some of my rage. I didn't work my way to forgiveness intellectually or even spiritually. It was in a dream. I was trying to kill him, but my methods kept failing. Finally, I had devised a method (I don't remember what it was), but I knew with absolute certainty it was going to work. Suddenly, I did not want to kill him anymore. I stopped whatever I had put in motion, and I did not kill him in my dream. When I woke up, I felt something in me shift. In my waking life I didn't want him dead anymore. I didn't even want him to suffer anymore. For me, that was forgiveness, and it set me free from some of the control of rage and revenge. I know that's not the kind of forgiveness a lot of church folks are talking about when they pressure survivors to forgive, but it was what I could do, and it made my life more manageable. For me, that was plenty enough.

Grace: Forgiveness was a long road. It is not easy to forgive someone who has tormented you. But I couldn't keep living with such a huge burden anymore. It was eating away into my body and my soul. I needed to forgive my perpetrator for my own sanity. But it took some time. It was a type of forgiveness that took me over a year to do. I struggled with it and whether it was the right thing to do as the perpetrator has not suffered any consequences from his actions. Instead, he just continued to live oblivious to his own hurtful actions. I really wanted him to reach out to me and confess his sinful actions toward me so that I could forgive. But I realized over time that this may not happen. So, in my internal struggle, I just needed to let go of this dreadful past and forgive for my own sanity.

Long before Andy Savage, however, in the 1980s popular televangelist Jim Bakker was accused of sexually assaulting a twenty-one-year-old PTL Club church secretary, Jessica Hahn. He argued that the sexual contact was consensual, and, to keep her silent, he gave her $200,000 in hush money. Hahn called the experience sexual assault, which affected her emotionally, psychologically, and physically. She could not believe that Jim Bakker, a man she admired, had done this to her in a hotel room in Clearwater, Florida. The sexual assault was organized by John Wesley Fletcher, who became a defrocked Assemblies of God minister. This public exposure of the sexual assault eventually led Jim Bakker to resign from PTL.[3]

Not all abusive pastors face Bakker's fate, as we see in the case of Andy Savage. His embrace by his congregation focused on the vertical understanding of forgiveness and did not seek transformation in the horizontal relationship with the victim. Savage did not feel the need to receive forgiveness from the person who he sexually assaulted or try to make things right again. Forgiveness from God seemed to "cover" the need to ask for forgiveness and to make restitution to the victim.

This form of cheap grace has been detrimental to victims, who continue to suffer for years after an assault. In fact, they are often blamed for the man's transgression and ostracized if they refuse to forgive their perpetrator. Rather than focusing on the perpetrator, the church needs to move victims to the center, recognizing that forgiveness is not a magical formula to allow perpetrators to move on without accountability to the wronged victims. Forgiveness is not cheap; it is costly because it requires both penitence and restitution. Without restoration for the victim, forgiveness cannot happen. The church must confront its troubling beliefs about forgiveness if it truly desires to support survivors and work to end sexual abuse. From the perspective of survivors, we learn that forgiveness must include restitution and transformation; the horizontal relationship with the survivor as well as the vertical relationship with God must become part of the church's understanding and practice of forgiveness.

Submission

Belief in women's submission reinforces their status as secondary, which gives men much greater authority and credibility than their accusers when survivors allege harassment, abuse, and assault. When beloved women's evangelical leader Beth Moore, who herself believes in women's submission, dared to challenge evangelical sexism and support for presidential candidate Donald Trump in light of his mistreatment of women, evangelicals turned on her. They stopped buying her publications, and later, when Moore jokingly tweeted she was preaching on Mother's Day, evangelical pastor John MacArthur said Moore should "Go home."[4] Complementarians claim to believe in women's equal worth with men but maintain that God has ordained gender roles that require women's submission—yet, when Southern Baptists passed a resolution opposing women in ordained ministry, part of their reasoning was that Eve was "first in the Edenic fall,"[5] thereby sentencing all women to subordination because of her sin, her unreliability, and her sexuality. Biblical interpretation plays a vital role in how we view and treat women and even how we understand sin came into the world. Despite biblical scholarship to the contrary, much of the church continues to blame Eve for the downfall of humanity. This blame then attaches to all women and becomes a justification for the subordination and mistreatment of women.

Southern Baptist leader Paige Patterson once told the story of a woman he sent back home to her abuser.[6] After she showed up at church battered and bruised, she asked Patterson if he was happy now. When he saw that, for the first time, her husband had come to church, he said he *was* happy—because now her husband had come to church. Here, Patterson has no regard for the well-being of the victim as long as the abuser attends church. Evangelicals tend to believe that life after death is more important than the present life. That means "winning someone to Jesus" is much more necessary than ending sexual violence or protecting a victim. The perpetrator's eternal life takes complete precedence over the present, real life of the victim.

An evangelical leader once told Susan that she had counseled an abused woman to go back to her abuser, commenting that if he killed her, which she admitted would be sad, it would be okay—because this woman would go to heaven, and her faithful witness might convince her husband to be saved. This response is common. Leaders often counsel Christian women, encouraging them to believe their reward for submission and obedience will be great in heaven, and all the better if their faithful witness wins their abusive partner to Jesus. For many believers, heaven and earth are completely separate. Heaven is a desirable place, but earth isn't. It's just a temporary stop on our way to eternal life. What happens to us on earth doesn't really matter; it is what happens in eternity that matters. This dualistic thinking overrides the possibility of having "heaven here on earth" or seeing the "kingdom of God" as something on earth. This single focus on eternity often means the church overlooks the harm right in front of them in favor of the sweet by-and-by. In this dualistic thinking, the only thing that really matters is if someone is "saved." Everything else can be sacrificed to this end—including the well-being, their safety, and lives of women, children, and LGBTQ people.

Many Christians define salvation, getting "saved," as praying a simple prayer asking for forgiveness and inviting Jesus into one's heart. It does not require accountability for past wrongs or a need to make things right. Worse, it sets a pattern for future sins that only requires the perpetrator to ask God for forgiveness, not to make reparations for harm done, much less to change the relationships of power that make abuse possible.

> *Sara: Sacrifice was expected. Especially of women. This was certainly what was modeled for me. The highest form of piety was to sacrifice. I really carried that with me . . . I think I realized that my deeply strong aversion to marriage—the whole hetero-normative thing, having children, becoming a mother—was because I had internalized the idea that those roles were inher-ently sacrificial. . . . It was so heavily part of my family life and what was modeled for me. I think it is still a dynamic in my family where I, as someone who is not married, does not have children, has been very focused on my career, and rejected the idea of sacri-fice and that as my role, I feel like the prodigal child. Not being willing, whereas my sister didn't feel the same pressures. She wanted to get married and have children and is working through her own stuff. My mother recently turned eighty. My father threw a big, lovely birthday party for her. He put together a speech about her life. One of the things he talked about was how she showed love for him by sacrificing for him. Afterward, my sister was just steaming over that.*

In the wake of #MeToo and #ChurchToo, some Christian men who have harassed and assaulted women have lost positions of prominence: Bill Hybels, pastor and founder of Willow Creek Community Church, resigned even while denying allegations of years of sexual harassment and misconduct. These allegations were credible as they were not based on any one accusation or accuser, but on collective testimony.[7] The church board had not provided effective oversight of the pastor, and, in fact, internal reviews repeatedly cleared Hybels of allegations of bullying and sexual harassment. Church leaders initially reacted nega-tively to women who made allegations and defended Hybels, calling the allegations lies. Hybels's resignation is an easy way out as he can keep denying his role as an abuser and not be held accountable for his actions. There is no need to ask for forgiveness as he continues to deny all accusations.

Paige Patterson was fired as president of Southwestern Baptist Theological Seminary when trustees learned that he had twice prevented women students from reporting sexual assault to the police, including telling a campus security guard to leave him alone with one student so he could "break her down" so she wouldn't report.[8] Ironically, he was almost immediately hired to teach ethics at another theological institution.

In 2019, the *Houston Chronicle* published an exposé on abuse in Southern Baptist churches.[9] The *Chronicle* documented at least seven hundred cases of women being abused over twenty years and found that abusers faced few repercussions. A blistering 2022 investigative report commissioned by the Southern Baptist Convention found that the SBC had engaged in a pattern of ignoring and covering up abuse.[10] Although the Convention eventually adopted rules to make it easier to expel churches that don't address abusers, many survivors have been unsatisfied with the denomination's limited response to the problem. Messengers to the 2023 meeting of the Southern Baptist Convention were supposed to address the problem of clergy abuse. Instead, they spent their time reaffirming the ouster of two churches that had ordained women as pastors and beginning the process to amend the denomination's constitution to exclude churches that affirm or call women as pastors.

In late 2020, news broke that deceased evangelist Ravi Zacharias had sexually abused and raped women over a number of years.[11] A member of the Christian and Missionary Alliance denomination, Zacharias preached all over the world, including at a Billy Graham conference in Amsterdam in 1983. He published more than thirty books and hosted two radio programs. His history of abuse did not come to light until four massage therapists came forward claiming he had behaved inappropriately.

Celebrated Canadian religious leader Jean Vanier founded L'Arche in 1964, an organization that runs homes and centers where people with and without disabilities live together. L'Arche operates in thirty-eight countries and has around ten thousand members. When Vanier died at the age of ninety in 2019, six women in France came forward accusing him of manipulative emotional and sexual abuse which occurred in the context of giving spiritual guidance.[12] The accusations sent shock waves through the Christian community worldwide. That the abuse happened under the guise of spiritual guidance makes Vanier's crimes especially devious and abhorrent—yet not uncommon. Many women and children have been emotionally and sexually abused by predators who have used counseling and spiritual support as a cover for violence. Many clergy groom their victims. They begin by showing emotional and spiritual support. Once they gain trust, they begin to abuse victims emotionally, sexually, and spiritually.

John Howard Yoder was a Mennonite scholar, ethicist, and one of America's more influential and admired pacifist theologians. During his twenty-four years of teaching at Anabaptist Mennonite Biblical Seminary, he abused more than one hundred women. What makes Yoder's actions even more sinister is that he carried out his abuse under the guise of religious experiment and theological study. Yoder admitted that he had interactions with young women in closed-door meetings, with hand-clasping, lap-sitting, and kissing. He engaged in partial disrobing, total disrobing, touching of genitals, and exploration of partial arousal. Others reported intercourse with Yoder.[13] Yoder called these "nongenital affective relationships" and suggested that "touching a woman could be an act of 'familial' love, in which a man helped to heal a traumatized 'sister.'"[14]

Yoder still emerged from all these sexual allegations as a model of repentance. His victims and accusers never spoke publicly, and their anonymity made it easy for people to push their allegations away. Yoder underwent a supervision and counseling process that saw him welcomed back into the Mennonite fold without ever taking full responsibility for his betrayal and abuse of women. Despite his legacy of harm, Yoder survived his scandal unscathed and forgiven.

In 2020, Jerry Falwell Jr., son of the late founder of the Moral Majority and president of Liberty University, Jerry Falwell, lost his job because of a sex scandal. He and his wife had a relationship with a young man they met in Miami, and he posed with his pants unzipped with a young woman whose pants were also unzipped.[15] Carl Lentz was pastor of megachurch Hillsong NYC until November 2020, when he was fired for a series of sexual affairs.[16] After that, news broke showing a culture of inappropriate relationships by staff members at the church, some of which included verbal, emotional, and physical abuse.

The pattern of abuse in Christian churches suggests the extent to which some Christian thinking about gender and sex creates a culture ripe for sexual violence. Although #MeToo and #ChurchToo have raised awareness of the extent of the abuse, few real structural changes have yet been made to transform the culture. In fact, many people seem to be tired of hearing about harassment and abuse, including church folk.

Misinterpretation of Scripture

Scripture has been misused to legitimize a lot of evil in the world. Scripture has been used to go to war, engage in genocide, colonize other nations, practice enslavement, justify racism, and abuse women and children. Chung Hyun Kyung once said[17] that the Bible needs to come with a warning label much like cigarettes do. At the front, it should state that reading the Bible may cause xenophobia, slavery, war, genocide, racism, and sexism. And this is exactly what has happened due to the misinterpretation of Scripture.

Christians who hold power, especially straight white men, have misinterpreted Scripture from the pulpit, from the church boardrooms and in the home, to rationalize their own power and maintain the status quo. In particular, Scripture has been used to subordinate women and children, dehumanize LGBTQ people, excuse men's misuse of power over others, and justify sexual abuse, assault, and rape. We need to divorce ourselves from white patriarchal misinterpretations of Scripture and reread scripture in light of context and survivors' experiences and with a lens of decolonization and liberation.

Biblical feminist scholar Elisabeth Schüssler Fiorenza reminds us that the central symbol of the gospel is *basileia*, or the kingdom of God. This word has monarchical and patriarchal connotations, but Fiorenza reminds us that, as a feminist vision, the *basileia* calls women to wholeness and selfhood. It can be a place of emancipation.[18] This is the new vision that we need to hold onto and not the patriarchal understanding of the kingdom of God.

As survivors of sexual violence, we need to be reminded of passages which promote equality. Paul writes, "There is neither Jew nor Greek, there is neither slave nor free, there is neither male nor female; for you are all one in Christ Jesus" (Galatians 3:28). This passage affirms the full equality of people, and therefore, one should not dominate or subordinate another person or group of people. Women are valued and equal to men. Women's bodies are just as important and wholesome as men's bodies. LGBTQ people are of equal value, and their bodies and selves, too, are deserving of dignity and respect. We need to recognize the gifts of gender and sexuality and celebrate and not violate or diminish difference.

We need to look to interpretations of Scripture from women, BIPOC, and LGBTQ people, interpretations that work toward liberation and flourishing of all people. We cannot keep using Scripture to view women and others as second-class citizens and use Scripture to legitimize violence, abuse, and assault against women, children, and LGBTQ people. We need to incorporate intersectional readings and liberative understandings of scriptures.

Backlash

Not surprisingly, a backlash to #MeToo has emerged. A September 2018 *Economist* poll found that, nearly a year in, Americans were actually more skeptical, not less, about sexual harassment, and this was especially the case among Republican voters.[19] Quickly after #MeToo and #ChurchToo emerged, another thread, #NotAllMen, tried to derail the #MeToo movement by shifting the focus from women's oppression to men's protection. Of course, long before the hashtag, feminists had often experienced this response when discussing the gendered nature of sexual harassment, abuse, and assault.

The hashtag misses the mark on many fronts. #MeToo has never accused "all men," but it has raised awareness of the culture of patriarchy and violence which feminists have named "rape culture." In this culture, violence, especially sexual violence, against women (as well as transgender and gender-nonconforming people and men who do not fit with society's expectations of masculinity) comes to be seen as normal through media, law, education, and theology. Whether or not all men assault women is not the point. The hashtag is a distraction from the larger cultural realities that most women, many men, and many LGBTQ people have been sexually harassed or assaulted, and most of those assaults are at the hands of men.

This culture manifests itself in things like "locker-room talk," the shared experience of men demeaning women as a masculine bonding experience. Men who do not actively engage in locker-room talk still participate as silent bystanders if they listen and do not intervene. Rape culture also shows itself in normalized inappropriate behaviors that seem to get a pass—commenting on women's appearance, coming on strongly to ask for a date or sex, putting a hand on a date's thigh and moving it upward without permission, wolf-whistling, and watching women sexually violated for entertainment in TV and movies, to name a few examples.

Purity culture is notorious for not only giving men a pass on these behaviors but actually blaming women for them. The 2021 Atlanta spa shooter was immersed in purity culture that made him feel guilty about sex. In response, he killed six Asian women spa workers to remove them as a temptation to him. In her memoir, *Pure: Inside the Evangelical Movement That Shamed a Generation of Young Women and How I Broke Free*, Linda Kay Klein explains how purity culture makes girls and women responsible for men's sexual weakness. Girls and women are required to dress, walk, and talk in ways that do not make men "victims of female flesh." Men's sexual weakness is actually seen as a sign of their hypermasculinity.

> *Sara: What I have learned, and I have heard this in multiple places, is that people who grow up in purity culture, conservative evangelicalism, will end up in therapy and be describing different things to the therapist, and the therapist comes to the conclusion that they have experienced sexual assault. But the individual will not have experienced sexual assault. They will have experienced purity culture.*

The backlash to #MeToo positions men as vulnerable to women's false accusations, which is perceived as much more dangerous than women's vulnerability to sexual assault. One of our favorite Twitter threads demonstrates the fallacy of the backlash. One person tweeted, "If you have a son, make sure you buy him a note pad, a body camera, & a recording device. Give him a battery pack too so he can always protect himself with video evidence of every single encounter he has with a woman. Men aren't safe in America anymore. There is a war on men." Another tweeter responded, "I decided to just teach my son to respect women. Fewer things to buy."

Of course, within these conservative Christian cultures, boys and men who are sexually abused must also grapple with dominant notions of masculinity. As abused people, they are feminized, positioned as being weak "like girls." The constraints of masculinity make it especially hard for boys and men to come forward when they have been sexually abused. Church teachings about masculinity and morality can intertwine in ways that further harm abused boys and men.

> *David: The teachings of sexual immorality made me believe I was the one allowing sin to occur. And the indoctrination of SBC's version of manliness made me think it was my fault for not fighting off the abuse, even though I was an undersized twelve-year-old little boy vs. a full-grown adult male.*

The scope of the problem of sexual violence and our seeming cultural inability to grapple fully with it, especially in the church, suggests we need to listen more deeply to survivors, think more critically about how sexual violence works, and act more meaningfully in the church and in the world to change the structures of power that support abuse.

CHAPTER 4

God the Problem

Our images of God—those pictures in our minds, the language we use, and the names we call God—can make us or break us. This is the power of words and images. Our images of God can significantly shape our sense of self, how we feel about ourselves and others, and how we behave and interact in the world. If we imagine God as a wrathful judge, we may see ourselves as inherently flawed, always failing, and even unworthy. Or we may imagine that we too should be judgmental, quick to point out mistakes, unyielding and uncompromising in our zeal for righteousness. Many of the church's traditional male images reinforce notions of God as a controlling power-over, one who demands total surrender, one who judges and punishes, and one who destroys and kills. The impact of these kinds of images on survivors of sexual violence can be profoundly deep, making God part of the problem and part of what must be survived.

These images may unconsciously and indirectly promote sexual violence by relying on ideas of God as male, all-powerful, domineering, watchful, judging, and warring. If God is these things, then why shouldn't humans be as well? These images can also increase survivors' trauma by promoting guilt and self-blame, equating abusers' behavior with God's behavior, and pressuring for submission, surrender, and self-sacrifice. Critiquing these images is an important first step in reimagining a God who can help survivors heal.

The Male God

Susan: *God is not my father. Not my priest, not my pastor, not my master, not my lord, not my king. All of these images of God are male images; they are all rapists of someone.*

Grace: *The image of a white warrior male God was implanted in me from a young age. This was and continues to be a terrifying image of God as it promotes a God of fear, conquest, violence, destruction, war, and sexual violence. Warriors went into war to destroy communities of people and often raped the women. It was a horrible act of violence, dominance, and destruction. This image is not a salvific image of God but rather a fearful, terrifying, and vicious one.*

No one has seen God.

Despite human beings' inability to see God, we have not stopped trying to imagine God and how God is viewed and understood. Throughout history, people have continuously conceived and created God, and, in most times, they have created God in their own image.[1] Since men are more powerful and dominant, men have projected themselves onto God, and God has been understood to be male. Most of the world religions have perceived a gendered God, and in a patriarchal world this deity is male. But we must remember that this is occurring in a patriarchal world where the men who are in power get to decide and imagine who God is. This occurs to the detriment of women and anyone else who is subordinated and subjugated to men.

The image of God as male has so infiltrated our imaginations that most Christians actually believe God is male, figuratively and anatomically. The birth of God's son Jesus only reinforced the maleness of God. Our prayers and liturgies in church show how this maleness has infiltrated our weekly worship, our Bible studies, our meetings, and our fellowship. We pray the Lord's

Prayer, which is a prayer to a male God beginning with "Our Father, who art in Heaven." Our baptismal formula reinforces a male God as the minister or priest says: "I baptize you in the name of the Father, the Son, and the Holy Spirit." The benediction at the end of worship reinforces a male Trinitarian God, as the blessing is some version of "May the love of God the Father bless you, the grace of our Lord Jesus Christ keep you, and the Power of the Holy Spirit sustain you, now and forevermore." In Korean churches, it is very common for the minister as well as the congregation to pray to "Father God" and this term is used repeatedly throughout prayer, whether one prays in silence or out loud.

One survivor wrote this poem:

On Our Images of God

Our father who art in heaven, they say.
They, who have not known illicit glances and illicit touches.
They may cry "Abba" when they kneel in secret places.
They may long to be enfolded in the father's arms,
held close to his bosom, where is peace and rest.

But those of us who have known the fear of love deformed
dare not cry "father" for fear that he might come
and again pull us close, but too close and too long,
and enfold us again in the darkness of his arms.

The maleness of God reinforces patriarchal stereotypes of gender and men's superiority over women. Just as we worship and obey a male God, so should women worship and obey their male husbands. Male theologians across the centuries have constructed and defended a male God who fortifies male human supremacy. God's maleness becomes a reason women are excluded from the priesthood, because a woman cannot stand in the stead of God. The Sistine Chapel ceiling, painted by Michelangelo in the 1500s, depicts an old white male God who reaches out to a white man, and this kind of image shapes and influences the thinking of most Christians, to the detriment of women, children, LGBTQ people, and BIPOC.

> *Grace: Much of the world is patriarchal. In Asia, patriarchy is evident in day-to-day living. In some parts of Asia, when a baby girl is born, there is mourning in the house as they prefer boys over girls. In China, there was a saying: "It is more profitable to raise geese than daughters." In Asia, where the importance of family is emphasized and upheld, a son is essential in every household, as the family lineage is passed on by the son. This deep-seated patriarchal culture is extremely difficult to dismantle.*
>
> *This is the culture I grew up in. Patriarchy was present at the dinner table, where men and boys ate the best pieces of meat, and women and girls ate whatever the men did not want. Women had to obey men under Confucianism, and this obedience requirement was transferred to the church, where women listen to and obey their male ministers and do not question any of their teachings, behaviors, or actions. Women's obedience to men in the family, church, and society has often led to abuse, which frequently gets ignored or overlooked. The perception that God is a "Father God" only reinforces the patriarchal culture within churches and communities of faith to the detriment of women.*

For many survivors of sexual violence, these images of God look like their abusers. They are not comforting or loving and, in fact, may inflict more trauma and harm. Although for some survivors an image of a father in heaven may replace an abusive father on earth, for other survivors a father in heaven may just be a larger-than-life male with power over them and their bodies: one more father who demands submission and silence. One friend said she remembered praying, "Some father you are! Surely a decent father would step in and stop this stuff." Even if we imagine God is loving and kind, we still know in the back of our minds that He (and we use "He" purposefully in this context) has the power to be otherwise. The kindly father

God is also the God who metes out punishment, suffering, and death. Survivors of sexual violence know that their lives may well depend on pacifying their abusers. Survivors of domestic violence become very good at reading the moods of their abusers and trying desperately not to do anything that might "provoke" their wrath. Many Christians also spend their lives trying to placate God so He doesn't punish them with His wrath. One wrong step, they fear, and the all-powerful God will rain calamity down upon them.

This God who incites violence gave birth to the United States of America. Christian beliefs were used to justify colonization and genocide against Indigenous peoples in the so-called New World. Many European Christian immigrants accepted the teachings of Pope Nicholas V, which gave Christians permission to call people pagans if they did not profess Christian faith. This led to land theft through the "Doctrine of Discovery."[2] Through this doctrine, white Christians believed they could justifiably kill "pagans" and take their land as an act of faithful Christian living. For the first inhabitants of the Americas, the God of most Europeans was a violent and terrorizing God who desired their elimination and the transfer of their land to colonizing European Christians.

Furthermore, these images of God's violence permeate Christian belief and are actually often presented as very positive. Susan was an English major who loved seventeenth-century British poetry, especially that of John Donne. She remembers in her prefeminist consciousness, however, still being deeply disturbed by one of Donne's sonnets in ways she couldn't articulate at the time:

> Batter my heart, three-person'd God, for you
> As yet but knock, breathe, shine, and seek to mend;
> That I may rise and stand, o'erthrow me, and bend
> Your force to break, blow, burn, and make me new.
> . . .

Take me to you, imprison me, for I,
Except you enthrall me, never shall be free,
Nor ever chaste, except you ravish me.[3]

Donne invites God to batter and rape him. He asks God to break him to make him new. In these images of God as batterer and rapist Donne describes God's power to overwhelm with violence, and he reinforces a notion that those who are battered or raped "asked for it" or "needed it." This theme of the victim "asking for it" has spilled over into a modern cultural narrative that rapists use to protect themselves from being charged with sexual assault crimes.

Similarly, a nineteenth-century Baptist hymn uses images of people needing to be violently controlled by an all-powerful God. It relies on the paradox that enslavement is freedom and death is life.

Make me a captive, Lord,
And then I shall be free;
Force me to render up my sword,
And I shall conqu'ror be.
I sink in life's alarms
When by myself I stand;
Imprison me within Thine arms,
And strong shall be my hand.
My heart is weak and poor
Until it master find;
It has no spring of action sure,
It varies with the wind.
It cannot freely move
Till Thou hast wrought its chain;
Enslave it with Thy matchless love,
And deathless it shall reign.[4]

Perhaps it should not be surprising to find this in a hymnal published by a denomination founded because of its support of slavery. If white people were willing to be enslaved by God, who would control them, then perhaps the enslavement of Black people was also necessary and justified since white people could not trust them to control themselves. African enslavement is almost viewed as a commandment from God to white people to maintain white social order and hierarchy. According to this thinking, humans need guidance and correction, even by the use of raw power. God's violence, like that of "benevolent" enslavers, is done to keep people on the right path because, left to their own devices, they will err. So, if need be, God can be enslaver, batterer, rapist, and abuser. These male-dominant views of God persist throughout Christian history, leaving a wake of harmed and traumatized people along the way.

The theological problem of God in regard to sexual violence starts with these images that are so deeply embedded in Christian thinking that many Christians think them literal. They take them at face value, rather than as the notions of people in a patriarchal place and time, grappling with their own understandings of God. They are also images that maintain patriarchy, for, as Mary Daly points out, "if God is male then the male is God."[5] The characteristics of men are projected on God, and then they justify the belief that men are more like God. Or, as one friend put it, "If God's a guy, he's doing a poor job of role modeling." What she's suggesting is that our image of God as a patriarchal male reinforces cultural stereotypes of patriarchal men that support and encourage sexual violence.

On the flip side, we project these stereotypes of human masculinity onto our images of God. In other words, images of men as violent and images of God as violent reinforce each other. Within patriarchy, maleness, whether a male human or a male God, means power, domination, control, stoicism, competition, and violence. Rather than the biblical idea that we are created in God's image (Genesis 1:27), we tend to create God in *our own* images. Our image of God is masculine, and it encompasses everything that is traditionally associated with masculinity: God is all powerful. God controls the world. God is impassive and unmovable. God demands loyalty and punishes disobedience. These characteristics of the male God then justify the system of patriarchy that supports and relies on sexual violence. It also tries to maintain the status quo which privileges men and whiteness.

The image of God as one who demands obedience is embedded throughout the Bible. In fact, some of the most troubling and distressing passages, as we'll discuss more in chapters 6 and 7, are those that require violence as an act of obedience. The story of Jephthah's daughter (Judges 11) is violent, disturbing, and agonizing. In this story, the judge Jephthah has just won a battle over the Ammonites and vows to offer the first thing that comes out of his house as a burnt offering to Yahweh. His only child, a daughter, sometimes referred to as Seila or Iphis, comes out to meet him, dancing and playing a tambourine (v. 34). Jephthah is shocked, as he expects an animal to come out of his house to greet him. When the daughter realizes what her father promised to Yahweh, she encourages Jephthah to fulfill his vow (Judges 11:36), but wants two months to weep for her virginity (v. 38). Shockingly, to fulfill his vow, Jephthah sacrifices his own daughter.

This story is dangerous on many levels. First is the notion that God demands a sacrifice, even a human sacrifice. This suggests that killing can be not just an acceptable form of obedience, but a required one. Second, Jephthah's willingness to keep his promise even after he realizes that the sacrifice will be his daughter indicates that a promise, an abstract idea, is more important than an actual human life and that violence is an acceptable means to fulfill the promise. This form of dangerous biblical interpretation and reading gets translated into real life when men continue to legitimize their violence toward women as "biblically sound" and as "biblical legacy/ tradition." We see this right now with some people calling for the death penalty for people who have abortions. Some people actually believe that violence toward women is necessary and is a direct commandment from God. Women are subordinate to men and therefore men have every right to do what they wish to discipline, train, and guide women through life's journey. Importantly, women are conditioned to submit to and even help with this violence against themselves.

Pastoral theologian John Poling argues that even a benevolent father is a father nonetheless, leaving the "patriarchal structure of the relationship . . . fully intact." In Poling's reading, this image of God means that the all-powerful father decides "unilaterally" to rescue His children who are helpless without His intervention. "The children are morally corrupt until they are saved by the perfect God," he writes. "The unilateral power relationship between God and humans is fully maintained. God has the power to be abusive, but God freely chooses instead to suffer in response to the evil of creation."[6] Theologian Karen L. Bloomquist argues, "Rationally we know God is not male, but 'He' still provides the security and order that many seek, thereby justifying the use of violence to maintain that order."[7]

A survivor wrote:

Doxology

> *Not words, nor tears, nor prayers*
> *for No One listens*
> *No One cares.*
> *This is my father's world.*
> *No healing comes for wounds that bleed.*
> *I only want.*
> *I only need.*
> *This is my father's world.*
> *No balm can soothe; not touch can heal.*
> *I no longer love.*
> *I no longer feel.*

This is my father's world.
    Long ago, a child once cried.
    No One came
    and something died.
This is my father's world.
    So no more words, no more tears.
    Possess me, Doubt.
    Destroy me, Fear.
Praise father, son and holy ghost.

God the powerful male is like the emperor image from the time of Jesus. Caesar was the emperor of the Roman Empire in which Jesus lived, ruling with power, authority, and ultimate force. At that time Caesar was "lord and savior," and claiming these titles for anyone else would have amounted to treason. Since there was no separation of politics, economics, and religion at that time, it would not have been an option to believe that Caesar was the political lord and savior and Jesus was the religious one.[8] Thus, Caesar was viewed as God. This authoritarian, all-powerful emperor image became intertwined with images of Jesus, and the white patriarchal church gradually transformed Jesus into an all-powerful, white authoritarian savior. This view of Jesus was then transferred to God, and is still prominent today in our churches, faith communities, and even our own families, despite the Bible's own witness to Jesus's life and ministry which were characterized by love, justice, mercy, and grace.

We don't think twice about the implications of this male image of God as it has become so embedded into our church language and belief system. We actually use these images as they are "truth." Many of us do not question what is taught in Sunday school when Sunday school teachers use masculine pronouns and images for God. We sit unconsciously absorbing male images of God in our Sunday prayers, liturgies, and sermons.

At what cost? Sociologists talk about how institutions "reproduce" themselves. In other words, people and institutions tend to like to keep things the way they are. So, they set up structures that do just that. For example, the dominant culture in the United States values the "nuclear family." So, society is set up to privilege the nuclear family so it continues to be the dominant form. Think about the images we see of families on TV or in the movies or the expectations we have that everyone has a father and a mother and that all adults have children that they raise with a spouse. Or think about taxes, forms, insurance, inheritance laws—all of these assume a nuclear family, and so the nuclear family reproduces itself. Similarly, the church reproduces itself as a male-dominated institution through its teachings, rituals, and roles. So, because the church has been mostly led by men, the church continues to be led by men. Because the church on the whole has subordinated women, it continues to subordinate women. Because the church has to a great extent served the interests of powerful white men, it will continue to serve those interests. Images of a powerful and violent white male God play a necessary role in this process by encouraging all people to accept the dominant view of white male power and the inferiority of all others.

This process of reproducing continues until something new disrupts it. In the United States, government was a white men's affair until abolition, the suffrage movement, and the civil rights movement disrupted it. We know, however, that although laws changed so that BIPOC and women could vote and hold office, even now we have to maintain activism to ensure access to voting to try to reach parity in representation in government.

In the church, new ideas and movements occasionally disrupt the church's reproduction of itself. The Protestant Reformation, for example, brought about great change in theology and church structure. Still, patriarchy remained a firmly entrenched feature of Christianity in both the Catholic

Church and Protestant churches. Feminist movements have created disruptions that have allowed women entrance into ordained ministry in some places, and yet we have not seen a thoroughgoing dismantling of patriarchy in the church. Instead, in many places we're seeing a retrenchment into patriarchy (purity culture, the Vatican's continued rejection of women in the priesthood, Southern Baptists' 2023 expulsion of a church that called two women as pastors on staff).

From the perspectives of survivors, we recognize that the church needs a thoroughgoing reformation. As it stands, the church on the whole perpetuates misogyny, gender inequality, homophobia, and sexual abuse through its promotion of male images of God, its demand for women's submission and exclusion from leadership, its vilification and control of women's sexuality, and its condemnation of gender and sexual diversity. Patriarchy justifies hierarchy, power-over, inequity, and injustice by linking God's power with men's power. We see this especially in images of God's violence that validate and excuse abusers' sexual violence.

The Violent God

Much of what we learn of God in church focuses on God's violence, from forcibly removing the first humans from the Garden of Eden, to asking Abraham to sacrifice his son, to commanding genocidal wars, to slaughtering the firstborn of the Egyptians, to threatening death and eternal punishment. Yet we almost always hear no critique of this violence; rather, we assume that because these are God's actions they must be just. From the perspective of survivors, however, these stories are a problem because they justify and sanctify incredible violence against all kinds of people. As survivors, we have to ask, is violence ok if God's the one being violent? Or do our experiences of God challenge unexamined acceptance of God's violence?

Grace: It is cruel, unimaginable, and difficult to comprehend these actions and commands of God. Some of these violent stories give children nightmares, as they try to read them as bedtime stories and have images of a violent and angry God in their imagination from a young age. I read the Picture Bible *as a child and then the* Picture Bible *comic book in my youth. The images in these books of a white male God's rage, threat, and anger toward the Israelites have forever ingrained in me a terrible violent image of the Divine who brings pain, suffering, and death upon humans and animals.*

As I grew up in the conservative evangelical Korean church, the male pastor and elders also acted out in anger and rage during church meetings and gatherings. When there were disagreements, I remember hiding behind my mother as I witnessed angry discussions and arguments flare up inside the church walls. These infuriating arguments were terrorizing to me as a young child. When it was all over, I heard many adults excuse these enraged behaviors as "all right" and "acceptable" since God was also an angry God, a God who didn't welcome sin or disobedience. These awful incidents from my childhood are still ingrained in my memory as if they just happened yesterday, and continue to instill in me fear of a violent and angry God.

These violent biblical stories have caused Christians to struggle with how they should understand and engage with a God who demands violent acts. They seem to contradict the stories and images of God as love and giver of hope, grace, and mercy. Commenting on the story of the flood, Poling observes, "The problem in this text is not just the evil of the creatures, but the destructive potential in the image of God. God has the power to create and the power to destroy."[9] In Poling's reading of this text and others, God's violence is a "constant threat to the creation."[10] In other words, creation is always in danger from the Creator.

Rarely are we encouraged to think critically about God's violence. We simply accept that because God is God then whatever God does must be righteous and good, even if it involves destroying entire peoples and killing God's own child. Susan recalls that in a seminary class when she rejected the idea that a God of love would order the wholesale slaughter of entire groups of people, a fellow student shouted at her that she, then, needed to "Get out!" of Christianity. For this fellow student, the God of holy war was as essential to Christian faith as any other doctrine. Somehow, God's violence was not troubling to the student because God was the one acting violently. God's status excused God for inflicting pain, suffering, and death, and, in fact, in the case of Jesus, it positively glorified it.

> Grace: I never really questioned the violence of the cross or the blood that was shed for me. We used to sing the hymn, "Are You Washed in the Blood?" and I never thought twice about what I was singing. I just accepted that the themes of death, blood, violence, and the cross were all part of the Christian church and Christian ritual. I never thought twice about whether it was the truth or whether it shapes how we view our relationship with God and ourselves.

Christians continue to glorify the death of Jesus on the cross. We sing hymns such as "Are You Washed in the Blood?"

> Have you been to Jesus for the cleansing pow'r?
> Are you washed in the blood of the Lamb?
> Are you fully trusting in His grace this hour?
> Are you washed in the blood of the Lamb?
> Are you washed in the blood, In the soul-cleansing blood of the
>   Lamb?
> Are your garments spotless? Are they white as snow?
> Are you washed in the blood of the Lamb?

We sing about the "old rugged cross" and a "fountain filled with blood." We ask, "What can wash away my sin?" and answer our own question with, "Nothing but the blood of Jesus." "What can make me whole again? Nothing but the blood of Jesus."

Perhaps nowhere is the violence of the male God more visible than in God's relationship to Jesus. Here the image is of a divine father who demands the suffering and death of God's child to appease God's own need for retribution (we'll return to this problem in chapter 8). The brutal whipping of Jesus, the painful crown of thorns on his head, and his sacrifice on the cross somehow cleanse us of our sins and make us all as white as snow. This cold-blooded murder of an innocent man becomes the "good news" for the whole world, a redemptive act for our salvation. This ugly, horrifying, and painful death is the pinnacle of the gospel story.

> *Grace: John 3:16 says, "For God so loved the world that he gave his only Son, so that everyone who believes in him may not perish but may have eternal life" (NRSV), and this passage, one of the first biblical passages I was introduced to, was one of my favorite verses.*
>
> *When I was a child, it felt like church and Sunday school revolved around this one biblical passage. We sang, prayed, and listened to sermons which all seemed to derive from this one passage. It was taught that the reason Jesus was ever on this earth was to die a horrific painful death so that we sinners could live eternally with God in heaven. The church preached how Jesus's suffering and violent death on the cross were all a necessary part of God's grand plan for humanity's salvation. This perpetual focus on the cross reinforced a violent God who demanded suffering from God's only son before God would forgive humanity. I accepted this as the truth and embraced this teaching deep down in my heart.*

Since God is all-powerful and God makes the rules, God is the one who decides that the wages of sin is death and that Jesus must suffer and die on the cross to pay that debt. Methodist minister Rebecca Ann Parker recalls her distress in reading Jürgen Moltmann's words in his book, *The Crucified God*: "God suffered in Jesus, God himself died in Jesus for us. God is on the cross of Jesus 'for us.'" She explains that this merging of

Jesus and God in Jesus's suffering felt familiar. "A merging of
father and son, named love, in which the father inflicts violence
on the child and then feels as if he were the one suffering, he the
one dying. . . . This is what the abuser does. God requires the
other to feel pain and then imagines the other is himself. God
finds life by lashing out with his pain and then embracing the
one he tortures."[11] This transaction, she says, ignores both the
suffering of the victim and the guilt of the abuser.

*Sara: . . . the big god that first kept me safe, but conditionally.
Right? I would be kept safe if I was obedient, if I was compliant,
if I didn't cause problems, especially for men and other people in
authority. And so, I learned, and was also very much concerned
about, not just about being a people-pleaser, but being an adult-
pleaser. I wanted other adults—I displease a whole lot of my peers,
and I was like "well, you don't matter, you're not in charge"—but
teachers, my parents, and anyone in a position of authority, I
wanted them to know that I was one of them. I would show that
by being not only obedient but diligent and even anticipating
certain needs and concerns. So, there was a lot of performative
perfectionism in my need to feel like I could be protected. Because
I felt like that was something that made me special. I was very
judgmental toward other people. I really wanted to be the person I
was told. God was reflected in all of these authorities. Phrases like,
"well done, good and faithful servant" were powerful to me—and
that obedience.*

Rita Nakashima Brock wonders why a loving being would use
violence to draw humanity closer. "Abuse," she says, "creates
intense emotional bonds, but they are the bonds of violated
boundaries, of broken hearts."[12] She says Christian theology
typically presents God as the parent, who is good, and humans
as the children, who are bad. These children are expected to
be grateful that God provides a way out of the punishment
that lurks behind God's benevolence. She writes, "This system

reinforces belief in the need for control and obedience, and fosters responses of guilt, relief, and schadenfreude" (pleasure at someone else's pain).[13] Brock also writes of the crucifixion of Jesus, "such doctrines of salvation reflect by analogy . . . images of the neglect of children or, even worse, making it acceptable as divine behavior—cosmic child abuse, as it were."[14] As decent human beings, we abhor parents when they physically abuse or hurt their child. It is illegal, and we are required to report abuse cases to the authorities. How then can we so easily let God off the hook for demanding a violent death for Jesus? Should God not also be accountable for God's actions and how God treats God's son? The image of Jesus being tortured for the rest of humanity and dying on the cross is violent and punishing, and this leads many feminists to rethink and reexamine his death.

Susan: As an evangelistic congregation, the church of my childhood believed that to avoid eternal damnation each person must repent from sin and make a personal commitment to Jesus as Lord and Savior. Every Sunday, our pastor preached a sermon that at some point focused on how to be "saved." At the end of every service, we had an altar call that gave people an opportunity to "walk the aisle," take the pastor's hand, and be led through a process to accept Jesus. The alternative to salvation was the eternal torment of the flames of hell, vividly described almost every week by the pastor. God is love, we were told, but God will also send you to hell for eternity if you don't do exactly as God says.

When I was six years old, a traveling evangelist came through town and preached at our church. I'd already heard many times how hell is hot and eternity is long. I'd heard about sinners who waited too long to repent and died before they accepted Jesus, only to wake up in hell for all eternity. So when this evangelist preached sermons full of hellfire and damnation, my imagination took over, and I started dreaming of going to hell.

The next Sunday, during the altar call, while the congregation sang, "Just as I am without one plea, but that thy blood was shed for me, O Lamb of God, I come, I come," I gripped the back of the

> *pew in front of me so tightly my little knuckles turned white. At last, I could live with the fear no longer, and so I slipped out into the aisle, walked to the front, took the pastor's hand, and told him I wanted to accept Jesus as my personal Lord and Savior, thereby sealing the deal to avoid the fires of hell (as Southern Baptists we believed "once saved, always saved," so that meant I was safe from then on, no matter what!). Somehow, by the time I was six, my church had convinced me that I was such a wretched sinner that I was deserving of hell. No wonder I was set up to accept sexual abuse from someone who was supposed to love and care for me. I had already accepted a God who was quite willing to send me to hell if I didn't do what I was told.*

God, the all-powerful parent, both sends suffering and then comforts us in the midst of it; God threatens us with hell and then welcomes us if we acknowledge God's power to do just that. And we call this love. Rebecca Parker calls this a "perverse love."[15] This is the pattern of abusers—to demand obedience, to punish with violence, and then to comfort and expect gratitude for it because we brought it on ourselves, and it's for our own good.

> *Grace: As a child of an immigrant, I was dropped off by my parents at different churches throughout the week. Looking back, I realized that my parents looked at this as free English classes for my sister and me. At the Baptist church on Sunday evenings, the old male pastor led the service with gospel songs, preached a fiery sermon, and gave an altar call. I always felt guilty during those calls as I felt like a big sinner who needed to be saved. On the days that I felt really guilty or sinful, I would answer the altar call again. I must have done this a dozen times or so as the church's teachings made me question my own salvation as I never seemed to be good enough to have eternal life. With doubts running through my young mind, I would answer and re-answer the altar calls.*
> *We also attended the Korean Presbyterian church on Sunday afternoons. During summer and winter breaks, there were many*

church retreats. There was always some activity to show what sinners we were and that was the reason God sent Jesus to die a violent death for us. This was always followed by an altar call. The altar call was done in a format that scared us into believing that if we didn't respond to it, we would burn in a hot flaming hell for eternity. There was a lot of fear instilled in us. After every one, I felt obliged to repent of my sins and take Jesus into my heart.

Black theologian James Cone points out that the cross can, on one hand, be healing but, on the other hand, can be very hurtful and painful. Cone writes, "It can be empowering and liberating but also enslaving and oppressive. There is no one way in which the cross can be interpreted."[16] If however, we understand that God required Jesus's death on the cross for humanity's salvation, then we have little room to imagine God as anything other than bloodthirsty, violent, and abusive. If we want to understand the cross in any way as healing or redemptive, we have to let go of the notion that God required a blood sacrifice, and reimagine the cross within a framework of love and justice, as we do in chapter 5. God's violence cannot be redemptive just because it is God's. Violence is violence, and it is always harmful.

God's violence reflects the sexual violence against women, children, LGBTQ people, and vulnerable men across the world. Within patriarchy, violence is evidence of strength, power, and control, and a violent God justifies violent men and their power over others. For survivors, a violent God is one more abuser, one more powerful being who inflicts pain and suffering because He can.

War as Sexual Violence

We can think of war as a form of sexual violence. How? People justify war by believing in the righteousness of God's violence against others. If God is violent, and we are like God, then we are violent. War is a grand-scale extension of this.

War emerges from patriarchal expectations of masculinity as violent. Governments, militaries, and soldiers use violence as a way to control or destroy others. War is an act of male power by nations, and those who carry out war (overwhelmingly men) enact male power over vulnerable individuals and groups—including women, children, LGBTQ people, men who do not conform to stereotypes of masculinity, Indigenous people, people in poverty, and disabled people—which among other forms takes the form of sexual violence. As an exercise in patriarchal power over others, war inevitably includes sexual assault and rape.

Although the early church was pacifist, in the fifth century, bishop and philosopher Augustine developed the idea, accepted by many Christians today, of "just war." Under certain specific conditions and with certain correct behaviors, a nation might rightfully wage war. Unfortunately, most of those conditions—such as making sure every other course has been tried before declaring war—are often disregarded today. And "just war" ignores the uncontrollability of violence when war starts and the ways it spreads, especially to vulnerable populations.

We also see biblical stories showing God demanding war and authorizing the genocide of entire peoples. Many contemporary Christians view biblical stories in which God commands the Israelites to go to war as justification for modern-day wars. So, for example, President George W. Bush claimed he was on a mission from God when he started the war against Iraq. Bush showed his religious fervor when he met a Palestinian delegation during the Israeli–Palestinian summit in Egypt which was four months after the US-led invasion of Iraq in 2003. Bush revealed at this meeting that God said to him, "George, go and fight these terrorists in Afghanistan." Then God told him, "George, go and end the tyranny in Iraq," and George obeyed and did.[17] Bush did not second-guess God's call for him to go and invade Iraq. To Bush, God is a warrior God and a God of war who engages in war for the sake of achieving peace. He really believed that God called him to invade Iraq and he only carried out God's call. For many people, like Bush, biblical stories of war justify engagement in contemporary wars.

Even as women have become soldiers, the image of a soldier is still rooted in masculine values and stereotypes. We expect soldiers to be stoic, powerful, and violent. We expect them to dominate and to win. Not surprisingly, we see high levels of sexual harassment and sexual assault in the military, experienced by over 6 percent of active-duty servicewomen and nearly 1 percent of servicemen.[18]

Militaries also use rape as a tool of war, such as the rapes of thousands of Mayan women by military forces during the thirty-six-year internal armed conflict in Guatemala (see chapter 1). Also, during World War II, the Japanese military kidnapped an estimated two hundred thousand young Korean women and made them into sexual slaves, called "comfort women," for Japanese soldiers (see Preface). They endured forced sex with hundreds of soldiers, contracted sexually transmitted infections, and those who survived were left with lifelong physical and psychological scars. Within patriarchy, these women were viewed as objects to be used and discarded, just like merchandise. (The Japanese government still has not publicly acknowledged their role in this horrific practice, nor fully compensated the few surviving comfort women.)

War also takes its toll on soldiers who are traumatized by their experiences in battle: by what they have seen, what they have done, and what has been done to them. Because men are supposed to be strong and violent, men who are traumatized often refuse to seek treatment, turn to alcohol and drugs to numb the trauma, or carry the violence into other arenas (such as their own homes). Images of God as a warrior or commander support militarization, war, and violence against civilians. Soldiers can be caught between following their individual consciences or facing the combined might of a violent military and a violent God.

If God is violent, human violence is justified, whether in war or in the home. Violence, as seen in God's actions, must sometimes be necessary to right wrongs, to enforce obedience, and to punish resistance. God's violence contributes to victims' acceptance of abuse—as their fault for being imperfect, as necessary to correct them, as God's will, as a way to teach them a lesson. If we must always submit to God, including to God's violence, then should we not submit to violence inflicted on us by those who represent God on earth—fathers, husbands, priests, leaders? And if we resist this violence, are we not sinning by not submitting to God's will?

If we believe God wills our suffering, we become willing to suffer and cause others to suffer, and even ask them to take responsibility for the suffering *we* have caused. How many children have been hit by a parent who said, "You made me do this"? How many women have been beaten by a man who said, "If you'd just do what I say I wouldn't have to hurt you"? If God is violent, what does it mean to say humans are made in the image of God? If God is violent, then do we accept that violence is an inevitable and even desired part of existence?

We will not end sexual violence without ending the violence of God, and we will not end the violence of God without ending God's maleness. For survivors of sexual violence, God's violence and the violence of their abusers can often merge. These understandings are all so entangled that we must rethink God's maleness and God's violence if we are to end it in our lives. A violent God cannot heal the wounds of violence for survivors. Rather, a violent God continues to perpetrate and enforce violence on survivors, and cannot create healing and wholeness.

The Damaged God

Experiencing sexual violence damages our view of God and often our ability to relate to and trust God. Traumatic experiences can shift how we think about power, privilege, evil, and the world. Where once we were trusting, sure of our ability to navigate the world, confident in who we were, sexual violence disrupts our sense of self, our confidence in ourselves and our ability to gauge situations, and our sense that the world is a safe and good place for us. For many of us already on the margins because of race, poverty, ability, sexual identity, or gender identity, sexual violence can reinforce messages that there's just something wrong with us. The trauma of sexual violence can cause us to question God as well as ourselves. The Damaged God is the God who did not protect us, who judges us, who has rejected us, and who possibly even caused our trauma to happen. This God is the result of those harmful images that permeate the church's language, teachings, and scriptural interpretations.

Laura: The abuse I experienced as a child drove me to God and church for sanctuary.

The spiritual abuse as an adult has driven me away from God and church. I have tried to not believe in Him, but I'm unable. My abandoning belief in Him feels like removing what little foundation I have. What else is there? Also, I've studied narcissism because of being spiritually abused and see some disturbing similarities with the character of God as I was taught by patriarchal, complementarian church leaders. I can no longer find solace in the phrase, ". . . though He slay me, I will yet praise Him . . ." Even Bible stories land differently, especially Old Testament ones— they piss me off! Attending church has been impossible for three years now. I cannot worship. Praying is useless—He's not listening anymore, it seems. I feel like I can't find Him.

Grace: I lay in bed crying and yelling, "Where is God in times of darkness?" When abuse is so traumatizing that you feel broken, alone and ashamed, you cry out to God and wonder where is God. In despair, I felt extremely lonely and abandoned by a harsh world, a pious church, and a male God. I felt that God who claims to love you and care for you didn't really care for me or protect me. I became damaged goods and therefore was not worthy of God's love, care, and grace. Instead, I felt that this male God allowed such abuse to happen to me. God felt cold and distant; God didn't care for my body nor my heart. I couldn't feel the presence of God, because if God is God, God would have protected me from sexual violence and harm.

Survivors of sexual violence may feel that God can't be trusted. After all, many of us have been told time and again that "God will take care of you," "God is in control," and "All things work together for good." Experiencing sexual violence makes those promises ring false. If God can allow abuse, assault, and rape, then how can we trust God to care for us? How can we trust God at all? Survivors of sexual violence may well feel God abandoned them at the very moment they needed God most, and platitudes like "Everything happens for a reason," "We can't know the mind of God," or "God will make something good of it" also ring false.

A survivor wrote:

The Silence of God

Darkness, you comfort me
by your familiarity.
Wrap yourself around me
like a shroud. Drown me
in shades of night. I'm never comfortable
in the light for long. I'm able
to see too much there. Here
I close my eyes against the world. I fear

only the fires of my soul which cast
light on my sepulchered heart. My mask
of death is no martyr's crown.
But for these demon whispers no sound
echoes through this tomb. This outstretched hand holds
no stigmata. Its fingers only unfold
from razor edge to pulsing blood
crying out against the silence of God.

If we believe everything that happens is the will of God, then God must be responsible for abuse. God either caused it or allowed it. This becomes a critical God problem. God joined in the violence either as an active participant or as a bystander who watched as we suffered. At the center of this image is a divine Father who commanded the abuse and death of God's own child, who in turn willingly suffered at the hands of his Father. This image makes suffering noble. It is God's will, and its model is Jesus. In this image, God is the Divine Abuser, the one who redeems us by suffering that parades itself as love. Furthermore, men use this image of a Divine Abuser as support for their own violent behaviors toward women.

Feminist theologian Rita Nakashima Brock believes that the patriarchal family embedded in Christian theology is part of theology's patriarchal assumptions.[19] These patriarchal assumptions continue to reinforce a father who is the head of the household and has power over all other members. The father can dominate over all others to the detriment of women. This understanding is easily transferred into Christian theology, which is embedded in patriarchal images and teachings.

Brock describes how atonement Christologies, which include original sin, expose how we become dependent on a father God to show us the way to a restored relationship with father God and with each other. The required punishment of one perfect child must occur before father God can forgive the rest of humanity. The death and resurrection of this one child is then celebrated as salvific and redemptive for all of humanity.[20] This horrific act of abuse of God's child has become upheld as one of the most sacred, important revelations within Christianity. This horrendous act of violence has become the basis of building a new religion, Christianity, which believes in the gruesome death of God's son as a path toward new life, salvation, and abundant life. If we can take a step back from this act of atonement, we recognize the brutality and violence of it all. But somehow this dreadful act has become the central message of salvation for all of humanity. This occurs if we continue to uphold and perpetuate a male, warrior, violent image of God which is contrary to the loving and liberative pictures of God found in our Scriptures.

Is there no other way toward salvation? What is at the core of divine nature that requires abuse, suffering, and death as the only way to divine approval? Why is God satisfied only by blood and death? This doesn't sound like "good news."

Ancient Israelites practiced animal sacrifice, according to the biblical text, at God's behest. Medieval Jewish philosopher Maimonides argued that God did not require animal sacrifice so much as use it to lure Jews away from pagan practices in which people sacrificed animals to feed the gods. Many Christians, however, have read these texts to suggest animal sacrifice for Jews was a mode of atonement that for Christians prefigured the sacrifice of Jesus on the cross. In this interpretation of sacrifice, God demands blood, whether animals' or Jesus's, to make things right. God's sense of righteousness has been insulted by sin, and the only remedy is violent death.

As watchful rule-giver and dispenser of punishment, God seems to be waiting for us to do something wrong. God, it seems, is just looking to get us, or perhaps God is "preempting" our sin by sending suffering to keep us from sinning, to teach us a lesson. Survivors carry a deep sense that we must have committed some sin to deserve our abuse, and we'd better be careful how we respond to it because we're being tested and watched by God. Sin lurks just around the corner if we don't respond in the one right way. Survivors often live with an overwhelming burden of guilt, shame, and self-blame for their abuse. We're also expected to forgive our perpetrators and are condemned if we don't.

Identifying God with maleness, power, might, and violence has damaged the relationship with God for survivors of sexual violence. This damaged God looks too much like our abusers, sides with them, and inflicts further trauma on us. God has little to offer survivors toward healing and wholeness. The damaged God continues to give power to abusers to continue their abusive actions and has for too long bolstered patriarchy, especially within the church. This damaged God needs to be named and recognized for what it is—a problematic view of God which only reinforces abusers' behavior and does nothing to comfort and heal victims of sexual violence. The damaged God has existed too long in Christian history without any challenge. It was simply accepted and worshiped as the true God. This damaged God has to go.

But as we discussed earlier, words are important as they shape our thoughts and ideas. These patriarchal words and images of God have already done great damage to women and other marginalized groups. We must do everything we can to fix this grave error so that survivors can find some source of empowerment, encouragement, love, and embrace from a nurturing and healing God.

We should look for other images of God to become part of a useful kaleidoscope of images that restore survivors and enrich their processes of healing. This is a required step if we are to move away from a damaged God. We must name God's violence in Scripture, center survivors' experiences, prioritize biblical images of God as love, and work toward liberation if we are to reimagine a God who helps survivors and who can offer comfort, encouragement, and healing. For too long, white men have defined God and upheld images of God which distorted our understanding of God and ourselves. This has been embedded throughout the two thousand years of Christian history. To undo two thousand years of patriarchal abuse, misunderstanding, and misportrayal of God will require us to drastically reimagine God, not only as a task for spiritual redemption but, even more importantly, as a task for earthly redemption in the here and now. Our goal should be to try to build a life-giving "kin-dom"—an inclusive community of all beings—of God here on earth. This community without violence is the good news, and, for survivors, it is a place of healing, solidarity, affirmation, empowerment, peace, and wholeness.

God's community is a lot like a diner—God's Diner. Singer-songwriter Carrie Newcomer has a song called "Betty's Diner." The chorus goes:

> Here we are all in one place.
> The wants and wounds of the human race
> Despair and hope sit face to face
> When you come in from the cold
> Let her fill your cup with something kind.
> Eggs and toast like bread and wine
> She's heard it all so she don't mind.[21]

Psychologist Alfred Adler developed a portion of his psychological theory on the notion (in German) of *Gemeinschafts-gefühl*. Loosely translated, it is the feeling of community, the sense of belonging. This feeling helps people feel they belong to the human race and are at home on the earth. They recognize their interdependence on others, their need for others' support, and their ability to support others. God's community is a place of *Gemeinschaftsgefühl*, a place of belonging, where survivors are at home with others and welcoming of others into the community.

You see, no one is turned away from God's Diner. There's no sign hanging on the door that says, "No shoes, no shirt, no service." No sign that says "Whites Only" or "English only spoken here." Susan's dear friend Paula was teaching at a conservative Christian college in California when the president stopped by her office to chastise her for not condemning homosexuality in her social work classes. Never one to shirk confrontation when she feels it necessary, Paula replied, "I am not the maitre'd at God's table. I don't get to decide who gets seated and who doesn't."

Survivors are welcome at God's Diner. God's Diner is always open and has plenty of seating. There's a story in Barbara Kingsolver's novel, *The Bean Trees*, that comes from Indigenous people of South America. If you go to visit hell, they say, you will see a room like a great kitchen. There's a pot of stew in the middle of the table, with the most delicious smell. All the people sit around the table, but they are dying of starvation. Why? Because they only have spoons with handles as long as mop handles. They can reach into the pot with their spoons, but they can't manage to put the food in their mouths.

Now, you can also go and visit heaven. There you see a room with the same table, the same pot of stew, the same spoons. But the people there are all happy and fat. Why? Because these people use their spoons to reach into the pot and then feed one another.[22]

In God's Diner, everyone gets fed. We're all fat and happy because we are a part of God's beloved community. It's no one's job to serve as bouncers for people who get too rowdy or wear the wrong clothes or love the wrong people or say the wrong prayers or struggle with trauma. The community's job is to go out into the highways and hedges and compel them to come in.

A banquet is set before us, the desires of our hearts, the psalmist tells us. And it is plentiful. There's no need to hoard or push anyone aside. In God's Diner, there's always more than enough, for the bounty of God is everywhere evident. And we are all welcome.

CHAPTER 5

God the Survivor

The story goes that a little girl in Sunday school was working intently on her artwork. Her teacher asked the little girl what she was drawing. "I'm drawing a picture of God," the little girl replied. "But," the teacher said, "no one knows what God looks like." "Well," answered the little girl, "they will in a few minutes."

Certainly, most people have their own ideas about what God is—creator, grandfather, spirit, mother, the man upstairs, omniscient, omnipotent, omnipresent. Theologians through the centuries have offered their fair share of answers—the Unmoved Mover, the First Cause, the Intelligent Designer, that Being than which nothing greater can be conceived, Creative Energy, Be-ing Itself. The Southern Baptist Convention says God is Father. The United Church of Christ says God is Eternal Spirit. When Moses asked God, "Who are you?" God said, "I AM WHO I AM." We're sure that cleared things up for Moses. And we are left with the same dilemma.

Most of us have no clue what we really mean when we speak the name of God. Many people respond by stubborn and closed-minded insistence on an entity that in most ways resembles an old white man wielding the power of patriarchy, refusing to entertain doubts and questions that might undermine the comfort of their security. Then there are folks like the two of us. We profess to believe in God—but we usually put an asterisk beside our profession. We are not comfortable with certainties, and we likely have more questions than answers. The paradox is, however, that we have passionately committed our lives to living as the people of this God we cannot explain and on some days cannot believe in the existence of.

God is ultimately more than we can explain or name, and so we begin with a dilemma of trying to explain that which is unexplainable. But don't despair. We do think we can make what poet T. S. Eliot calls "hints and guesses."[1] In physics, there are particles that scientists study that they cannot see. They study these particles by doing things and then watching what happens. So to study electrons, scientists shoot beams through atoms and then watch what happens to the beams. From the beam's reactions, scientists then develop hypotheses about electrons. Likewise, we can look at the evidence around us to find those hints and guesses about God. And some powerful hints and guesses can come from the experiences of survivors of sexual abuse.

Instead of an all-powerful God who causes or allows suffering, survivors of sexual violence can recognize God as the One who suffers and survives sexual violence with them. God is present in and experiences their suffering; God is their cosufferer and companion on the journey through violence and toward healing. Rather than being power-over, God is power-with and power-to. God is in relationship with survivors, affects and is affected by their suffering and their resilience. Developing images of God as coinhabiting survivors' suffering adds another dimension to our understanding of God as we imagine how God can inspire resistance and liberation.

The Suffering God

Susan: When I rejected the all-powerful God of my childhood who had either caused or allowed my abuse, I searched for another way of understanding God's involvement in what happened to me. Fortunately, I came across process theology, and it allowed me to let God off the hook. In process theology, God is not coercive power but persuasive love. God does not control the universe but rather calls each entity to choose to fulfill its divine aim. God did not cause nor could have stopped my suffering. I suffered because another human being chose evil and power over a child. So where was God? God was suffering with me. God feels with us. God exists in every atom in the universe and experiences what we experience, and so God suffered with me.

Grace: The traditional masculine God could not help me in my experiences of abuse and destruction. In my theological studies, I discovered that it is the God of liberation who can ultimately save me from the harmful and oppressive powers that dominate women. God is a loving God who seeks to set us free from harmful and unjust structures. The God of liberation seeks to heal us and bring wholeness to our bodies, hearts, and minds.

Traditionally, Christianity has viewed God as unchanging. Early Christian belief was deeply influenced by Greco-Roman philosophy, which argued that only imperfect things change and, since God is perfect, God cannot change. The ancient Hebrew idea of God was different. Exodus 3:14 is often translated as "I Am Who I Am" (NRSV), but a more accurate translation is "I will be what I will be." In other words, God becomes and changes. This perspective proves much more helpful as we imagine God, too, as a survivor.

If we look at suffering in this light, instead of seeing God as an unchanging being who is the same yesterday, today, and forever, we will recognize that God is affected by what happens to God's creation. Feminist theologian Elizabeth A. Johnson explains, "God takes the pain of the world into the divine being in order there to redeem it."[2] We can then imagine God as a young gay man dying, hanging on a fence in Wyoming, the result of a homophobic hate crime. God is a trans woman beaten to death, a Korean comfort woman, an altar boy abused by a priest, a physically abused woman in a confidential shelter, a single mom typing #MeToo on her Twitter feed. What do these images teach us about God?

> Grace: I was told that everything happens because of God; the good, the bad, and the terrible things. The terrible things included the abuse I endured. It was all part of God's purpose and plan in life. This teaching was so difficult for me to believe and accept as a young child. Why would God allow suffering to happen to young children? Why was I taught "It is all God's will, so just accept it"? This church teaching took me into deeper depression and turmoil as I tried to reconcile the loving God with a God who allows pain to happen. But pain cannot be overcome with a theology saying everything happens because of God. As I learned more about God, I learned that God is always with me, in my happiness, in my sickness, and in my suffering. God suffers along with me and is in my pain.

The traditional notions of a static, unchanging, and unmoved God do not work in the face of sexual violence. As we saw in previous chapters, these traditional notions of God implicate God in violence. By bringing an intersectional lens to our focus on survivors we can begin to see the myriad ways God is affected by and is present in suffering.

As we approach the question of the Suffering God, we want to ask, "How is suffering redeemed in the divine being?" James Poling notes that the emphasis on the Suffering God can be "highly problematic" because it encourages survivors to suffer their own abuse in silence. This suffering in silence happens often in Asian communities where shame prevents survivors from speaking out and sharing their experiences of abuse. The shame falls not just on the victim but on the victim's entire family. This burden of shame becomes an added layer of difficulty for many victims of abuse. The experience of shame also happens in Asian immigrant communities where immigrants often feel isolated and alone, and do not have access to supports, or means to seek help in abusive situations. Poling writes, "There is something wrong with an omnipotent God who encourages victims to suffer in silence for the evil of others."[3]

Rather, suffering is redeemed in God when God's liberative call empowers us to resistance, resilience, and justice. Suffering in itself is not noble nor redemptive; in process theology, suffering is evil because it damages our enjoyment, our ability to fulfill our divine aim. Suffering is not a characteristic of the human condition but a disruption of it. Process theology recognizes that some suffering is caused by the nature of the world—viruses, earthquakes, accidents. Other suffering is caused by the acts of human beings who choose to do evil—torturers, war criminals, bullies, harassers, abusers, and rapists. God's suffering with us is only redemptive if God joins with us in resisting those who perpetrate sexual violence.

A survivor wrote:

The Exorcism

No more,
no more,
demon of memory.
Legion,
I'll no more of you.
Your haunting images
which taunt and tease
will no more move me to tears,
no more wake me from pleasant dreams,
nor lull me into hellish nightmares.
I'll sit no more among your tombs
raving in fragmented thoughts with broken words,
no more hear your lying voice whisper guilt in my ears.
Away, Legion,
for you are many,
and I but one, though not alone.
No more, no more.

Kind hands and hearts have taken away your sting,
have stripped away your victory
and cast you into outer darkness
where you plunge headlong down the steep cliffside.

God suffers in our sorrow, pain, and misery. Recall the Korean word *han*, which we discussed in previous chapters. *Han* is a difficult word to translate, but we can think of it as deep and ongoing pain as a result of unresolved injustice or unjust suffering. Unjust suffering occurs when social systems are set up to create disparities and lack of access to resources. These systems—racism, sexism, heterosexism, colonialism, ableism, classism, and ageism—shape the foundations of our society and contribute to suffering that creates woundedness and pain deep in the heart. *Han* can be experienced by individuals, by a group, or by an entire country. During Japanese colonial rule after Japan invaded Korea and assassinated Empress Myeongseong (October 8, 1865) and then removed the Joseon Dynasty in 1910, Koreans as a nation experienced collective *han*. When a young girl is raped, she experiences extreme individual *han* and deep woundedness. This *han* can be passed on to future generations if it is not resolved or released by the person experiencing it. Therefore, it is essential we heal unjust suffering and pain and transform the systems of power that cause sexual violence.

When individuals and groups of people suffer unjustly and experience *han*, we may wonder where God is. God is not absent from us and unaffected by sin, but is with us and is hurt and moved by our suffering. God also experiences the sharp piercing of the heart caused by *han*. We do not suffer alone; God is always with us in the midst of our suffering, pain, and brokenness. When a young girl is raped, God suffers. When a woman is molested, God is there in the pain and suffering. Korean American theologian Andrew Sung Park states, "God suffers not because sin is all powerful, but because God's love for humanity is too ardent to be apathetic toward suffering humanity. No power in the universe can make God vulnerable, but a victim's suffering breaks the heart of God."[4] God suffers in Christ on the cross because of God's love for him and for humanity.

Much of Christian thought in the past did not allow room for a Suffering God due to the influence of Greco-Roman philosophy. Because God is perfect and unchanging, the argument goes, God is also impassive, unmoved by earthly events. If God is perfect and does not change, and God does not feel and is not moved, then God cannot suffer, as suffering requires change and feeling. Process theology and other liberatory theological movements challenge this idea of God as perfect and immovable. Rather, these theologies see God in every particle of the universe, intimately connected with everything, present with us and experiencing our pain and suffering.

When we focus on the Spirit of God, it helps us further comprehend how God is present in the universe, in all things and in every person. The Hebrew word for spirit, *ruach*, means the breath, wind, energy, and spirit of God. The breath of God is found in all living things as "the Spirit of God was hovering over the waters" (Genesis 1:2 NIV). When we think of breath and wind, we know it gives us life and makes things move. Breath and wind are forms of movement or waves or energy. All forms of life are made up of particles which vibrate and move. Nothing alive is static but is full of movement, action, and vibration. In this way, God's presence, which is in all life, continues to move and stir us. God is indeed in every particle of life in this entire universe and moves within all of creation. This is how we experience God's breath, wind, and movement, and God experiences our joys and sorrows, our celebrations and sufferings.

As a cosurvivor, God embraces the complexities of our feelings and responses to violence. God understands our rage, our depression, our will to fight, the days we can't get out of bed. God feels these things with us. Rather than expecting us to suffer in silence, God calls out for justice and stands alongside us in naming our abuse, resisting suffering, speaking out, and surviving.

None of this makes the suffering okay. None of this means we're better people because we suffered or that suffering taught us a necessary lesson. It means that, although our suffering broke God's heart, God works with us to create a world where no one else has to suffer. The world is redeemed, not by our suffering or God's, but by ending suffering.

God as Space to Grieve

We often rush to images of God as healer and think we show our faith by acting as if violence has had no lasting impact on us. But we know that healing from trauma is a process, and part of that process is grieving what has been lost. If we imagine God as space to grieve, we can experience God as a place where we can sit in relationship with One who has suffered with us and feel all the rage and sadness that accompanies trauma.

When we are broken by sexual violence, we need time and space to struggle, to grieve our loss, pain, suffering, and turmoil. In our pain, we can lament. Lament is a spiritual practice which we see in the Hebrew Bible, where the Israelites who have been treated unjustly turn to God in sorrow. Lament is a cry out to God from the pain that people have experienced. Lament can be individual or it can be collective. We lament before God for the wrongs that we have faced and endured. As we cry out to God, God hears us and provides comfort to us. God doesn't expect us simply to say a prayer, go to a Bible study, and suddenly feel happy and whole again. Sitting with our grief is not an expression of faithlessness but of faith that God can hold our grief and sorrow.

Space to grieve and not to hurry on is an important psychological stage. If we try to rush on to healing without grieving, we lose a natural step which actually brings inner and holistic healing. In God's infiniteness, we enter into an infinite space to grieve. There is no rush or hurry in this space provided by God. God is the creator of all things and in God's creative time, we grieve and experience our sorrow. We allow the pain of our sufferings to move through us and out of us. We need to grieve.

We grieve loss and grieve our abused and damaged bodies and psyches. As we grieve in God's space, we recognize the fullness of God's grace and love. We understand that as we grieve, the God who also suffers grieves with us. In that space, healing of our bodies and minds can begin to happen.

God the Child

Rita Nakashima Brock suggests we can imagine God as Child as a Child locates divine power in vulnerability and interdependence.[5] The Child moves us to identify with victims and God does come to us as a Child. God the Child is seen in a manger in Bethlehem, where divine vulnerability reveals itself, and God the Child is also seen in abused, violated, beaten, trafficked, and murdered children. In Trayvon Martin, Tamir Rice, a friend's teenage daughter who was abducted and trafficked, the child Susan once was, a baby in a manger whose parents had to flee their home country as refugees, we see a God who is vulnerable, who experiences suffering because of the actions of individual people and social institutions like police, family, and government. We see a God who understands broken bodies and broken spirits. But survivors are more than their abuse, and in God the Child we also find resilience and joy.

God the Child is full of wonder at their own creation. In process theology, the future is unknowable to God because the future is open-ended, depending on the choices of each person. At every moment, God calls each person to make their best choices, but God does not determine what choices are made, nor the consequences of those choices. That means God can be surprised by us. Like a child on Christmas morning, God can experience excitement and delight when we choose what is good and right. Imagine how boring things must be for the God of tradition, the all-powerful, immovable God who wills everything and knows all that will happen. God the Child offers God the joy of authentic and interdependent engagement with diverse people from whom God learns and experiences diverse ways of being in the world. God the Child takes in not only the suffering of children, but also their joy.

God the Child offers survivors encouragement to reclaim the damaged children within themselves. God the Child symbolizes how both suffering and joy can live side by side in damaged beings. Rather than asking survivors to "get over" their suffering, God the Child allows the "both/and" of simultaneous suffering and joy. Survivors do not have to reject the suffering children within themselves to experience joy; it's not one or the other. Rather, survivors can enrich their sense of joy by embracing the suffering child as an integral facet of their existence.

God the Child reveals the vulnerability of God who is susceptible to harm. God the Child does not abandon us in our suffering and pain but makes the choice of being with us in a broken world. God the Child who is vulnerable suffers in our pain as God experiences *han* and the piercing of the heart. God's vulnerability provides this open space for us to enter into God's realm as we suffer. We can find much comfort in knowing that God welcomes us into a place of vulnerability.

God the Child offers hope to us. When a child is born, they are born with the hope of the future. God the Child bears that hope for us, those who have been broken and trampled on and those who have suffered sexual assault. According to the prophet Isaiah, "For a child has been born for us, a son given to us, authority rests upon his shoulders; and he is named Wonderful Counselor, Mighty God, Everlasting Father, Prince of Peace" (Isaiah 9:6). Hope was wrapped up in God the Child who was born for us. This is the hope that we cling to during the suffering we face.

Hope becomes an anchor in our lives. Early Christians who were persecuted used the image of a fish or an anchor to reveal to others their Christian faith. Christ became an anchor for us and gives us grounding space for our lives and our faith to grow. Hope is not just some optimistic way of viewing the world; it grounds us to work toward justice. We live in hope that justice will come to abusers who commit atrocities and feel that they can get away with it all. Justice will bring peace to the victims of abuse who live with anguish, fear, and shame. Hope leads us to work for good in the world and to build the realm of God wherever we go.

God the Child also brings peace. Sexual abuse survivors feel turmoil that can last a lifetime. They crave something to provide peace for their suffering and anguish. God the Child who is the bringer of peace can provide the solace that many survivors seek. Jesus said, "Peace I leave with you; my peace I give to you. I do not give to you as the world gives. Do not let your hearts be troubled, and do not let them be afraid" (John 14:27 NRSV).

Finally, God the Child brings love. When a child is born, a baby brings so much love into the family. The love is reciprocated when the family shows love back to the baby. We can see love in God as God the Child brings love into the world.

God the Child also teaches the world how to love. In a broken world, we need to love the poor, the outcast, the marginalized, the sick, and the violated. We are to love those who are different from us, and we are to love those who are suffering and dying. We also need to love ourselves and the wounded beings we carry within us.

> *Susan: For a long time, I pushed her away, that child I was who had not stopped her abuse. I shut her down, shut her out, blamed her. When I was in seminary, I developed a friendship with the daughter of another student in the program. She was the same age I was when my abuse began. She was so young, and I suddenly realized how very young I was too when I was abused. I would never have held my friend's daughter responsible had she been abused, and so I started to wonder why in the world I was holding my younger self responsible. Then one day I was looking at a photo of myself as a young girl, and I saw the child I was. I was overwhelmed by compassion for that little girl, and for the first time I embraced her.*

> *Grace: I grew up in an Asian North American culture where the elders are the focal point of the community, and the child is not considered significant. Children were taught to obey parents and treat elders with the utmost respect. This included the church community, social community, and elders in the wider community. God the Child turns the Asian American world upside down and shows the community that respecting elders is important, but so is respecting the child. The vulnerable and hopeful child can show us how we are to treat the powerless in society, hear their voices, accept their truths, and welcome them into the community. We were all once children, and we should care, respect, and honor God the Child.*

The Relational God

James Poling asks, "What would it mean to devise an image of God who lives within the relational web as a fully active and inter-dependent partner with creation?"[6] Rather than thinking of God as an authoritarian figure with power over human lives, we can think of God as an active participant in mutual relationship with each person and the natural world. God is no longer the Creator who is a threat to creation but a loving collaborator in seeking healing, peace, and justice. God is a friend, a companion, a fellow sojourner who shapes and is shaped by relationship with each of us.

In Asia, relationships are central, and society is based and built on relational terms. A Korean word that helps us think about the importance of relationships is *jeong*. *Jeong* can be translated as "sticky love"—love that can't let go, much like fingers dipped in honey that are stuck together. *Jeong* is the love between people that is sticky like honey and therefore keeps the relationship together. In any relationship, people may argue, fight, and try to break the relationship, but *jeong* keeps the relationship unbroken and together. For example, friends may argue over something and get angry with one another. Sometimes friends may feel that they never want to see the other again. But somehow friends will stick together even after tumultuous times, due to *jeong*. *Jeong* is intangible, but the effects are strong as it holds people together and keeps relationships whole.

Jeong can be present in families, among friends, and among coworkers and neighbors. *Jeong* is a strong, binding love that holds society together and prevents it from shattering. As we move away from the authoritarian God of patriarchal European theology and toward a Relational God, we recognize and experience the deep unconditional love that God has for us. It is so strong and binding that it becomes a "sticky love" like *jeong*, which keeps us close to God and prevents us from breaking away from God.

We can see the Relational God more clearly in a Trinitarian (three-part) view of God. These three parts are seen as in relationship, a harmonious dance sometimes called *perichoresis*, a

Greek word that refers to encompassing, or revolving around. This word is used to show the indwelling nature of the Trinity, which is intimate and interconnected. Once used by the early Church Fathers, it is now used by modern theologians such as Jürgen Moltmann, who tells us that the three Persons of the Trinity (God, the Son, and the Holy Spirit) exist not just separately in the "common divine substance" but in relationship each to the other.[7]

The Relational God was present when the world was created, as God said, "Let us make humankind in our image" (Genesis 1:26 NRSV). The plural possessive "our" is used in Hebrew in this passage, highlighting the significance of relationships both within the divine being and between the divine being and humans. As the divine being is in a dance within Godself, God is in a dance with humans, and humans with one another.

Susan: Healing for survivors is a lifelong process. We don't just pray the pain away. Still, sometimes grace bursts in on us in unexpected ways. I remember once in my early thirties I was having a really difficult moment turning my abuse over and over in my mind. I distinctly remember sitting on the floor of my apartment crying, when I felt a palpable presence envelope me. She was definitely feminine, and She embraced me and held me like a Mother. For a brief while, we just sat like that on the floor, Her love wrapped around me. That moment didn't take away my struggle, but it reminded me so concretely that God was with me, not as divine power but as divine love.

Grace: During my seminary studies, I decided to seek the seminary chaplain to help me deal with the abuse I experienced during my childhood and youth. It was difficult to open up and share with someone and also trust that it would all be safe. I had several meetings with the chaplain, all ending in tears and anguish. Afterward, I would often go sit and pray in the chapel. The chapel had tall ceilings with a huge stained-glass wall behind the pulpit. It was a beautiful site for prayer and weddings. One day while I was praying in the chapel, I suddenly felt the warmth of a hug surround my body. It was the Relational God who reaches out to us in our times of suffering and pain and embraces us with love. It was the sticky love, like jeong, *which suddenly enfolded my entire body to give me an assurance that God is with me. God is with me in happiness and also in much pain and sorrow. I was certain of this that day.*

Making a Way Out of No Way

Delores Williams and Monica Coleman imagine God as the One who "makes a way out of no way" for Black women[8] and is concerned with their survival. Williams points out, "Physical violence done to black women was matched by emotional and psychological pressure put upon them."[9] She notes that often Black men, including the Black preachers to whom Black women turned for support, sexually exploited women. She says that despite the victimization and oppression of Black women, they have found a way to hold onto faith by experiencing God as the one who helps them survive when all options seem closed. Karen Baker-Fletcher calls this "making do."[10]

Drawing from the story of Hagar (which we also saw in chapter 2), Coleman is clear that making a way out of no way and making do are not necessarily liberatory; they are survival strategies that point toward justice, but may not attain it. The God Who Makes a Way Out of No Way provides "options that do not appear to exist in the experiences of the past."[11] The way forward, Coleman explains, is not in the past but lies in the unseen possibilities that come from God. God is the one who presents visions of new possibilities not seen before. Implied in making a way out of no way is a call to justice, because the suffering of Black women results from the social systems that target and harm Black women. God is the one who provides "possibilities that are not apparent in the experiences of the past alone" that open the way for decisions that "lead to survival, quality of life, and liberation for black women."[12]

Victims of sexual violence may find themselves with limited options and resources for support, healing, and thriving. Feeling isolated, violated, exploited, and hurt, they may find themselves in a situation where they feel there is no way out. In some cases, suicide seems like the only option. Many Korean comfort women who were kept as sexual slaves committed suicide by jumping off cliffs. More than one-third of women who have survived rape contemplate suicide at some point after the assault. Survivors of sexual assault are more than ten times as likely to attempt suicide than people who have not been sexually assaulted.[13] Too often, survivors feel that there is no way out of the shame, guilt, fear, and depression they carry following sexual violence. But as Black women show us, for survivors God can be the One Who Makes a Way Out of No Way. A God who cares for the survival of victims of sexual violence offers hope for a future beyond the devastating consequences of violence, in which survivors can create healing, wholeness, and joy.

The Mothering God

Mothering is something people of all genders can do when they offer love, support, nurturance, and guidance to others. Therefore, simply replacing images of God the Father with God the Mother may be counterproductive. After all, earthly mothers, like earthly fathers, can let us down. Mothers can exercise power-over and abuse. "Mother God" as a theological image also reinforces a gender binary that assumes women give birth and then by virtue of their gender nurture and care for their children. Instead, we see "mothering" as action rather than being.

The Mothering God gives birth to us and gives us life. The Mothering God nurtures us and provides shelter when we need it. Luke 12:34 says, "How often have I desired to gather your children together as a hen gathers her brood under her wings, and you were not willing!" (Luke 13:34, NRSV). As a hen gathering her brood, the Mothering God protects us under her wings. When we feel alone and broken, God provides shelter for our brokenness, loss, and suffering. Those who suffer from the effects of sexual violence can turn to the Mothering God to wrap us in her arms to provide everlasting love and support.

In the Hebrew Bible, the Spirit is written in the Hebrew feminine as *ruach*, who brings forth life in creation (Genesis 1:2). In the New Testament, *pneuma* is the Greek word for the Spirit who gives forth life. "But if Christ is in you, though the body is dead because of sin, the Spirit is alive because of righteousness" (Romans 8:10). The Spirit is present at the conception of Jesus and his baptism (Luke 1:35, 3:22). "Semitic and Syrian early Christians did construe the divine Spirit in feminine terms, attributing to the Spirit the motherly character which certain parts of the Scriptures had already found in Israel's God."[14] The Spirit gives life and is the creative and maternal God who brings forth the birth of Jesus and the new members of the body of Christ. The Spirit God moves us away from traditional patriarchal notions about God and moves us toward a wholistic, all-embracing understanding of God. The Spirit God does not exclude people, but welcomes everyone, especially those who are hurt and suffering.

The Mothering God is also a fierce protector. Deuteronomy tells us that God is a mother eagle protecting her young under her wings (32:11–13), and Hosea depicts God as a mother bear bereft of her cubs (13:8). For survivors of sexual violence who have felt incredible vulnerability and helplessness, the image of the protective Mothering God can offer solace against the disappointment in those who failed to protect survivors. Of course, this image is complicated because we know God does not intervene in human events and protect from sexual violence. Instead, this image allows us to see God as the one who joins with us in protecting our own humanity in the face of sexual violence. The Mothering God helps us hold onto a sense of self-worth and value, even if we have been violated. The Mothering God suffers with us and, in our suffering, reminds us that we are loved.

The Mothering God is also fierce in her demand for justice. *Hokmah* (Wisdom) "cries aloud in the street, in the markets she raises her voice; at the head of the noisy streets she cries out; at the entrance of the city gates she speaks" (Proverbs 1:20–21). Again and again, the Bible puts justice at the core of God's desire and demand. The injuries of sexual violence cry out for a justice that both makes the individual situation as right as possible and transforms the oppressive systems in which sexual violence flourishes.

We seek the Mothering God during our times of need, brokenness, and pain. The Mothering God will bring healing and bring forth new life in our damaged bodies and souls. We bear the biblical hope that life comes anew through the Spirit of God. The Mothering God nourishes our damaged bodies, renews our broken spirits, and with us seeks justice.

The Queer God

"Queer" means at odds with what is "normal." As a sexual and political identity, queer is a challenge to heteronormativity (the assumption that everyone is heterosexual ("straight") and the ways society is built on and reinforces this idea). For example, how often do we assume everyone has a mother and a father? Why do people not have to "come out" as heterosexual? Why are LGBTQ people, especially trans women of color, at great risk of violence? Imagining God as queer disrupts heteronormativity.

We imagine that for many people even the suggestion that God is queer is shocking (remember, Sallie McFague says the best metaphors for God give a shock). But it's only shocking because, while we know God does not actually have a sexual identity, we still assume God is straight. The straight white male God is the norm throughout most of Christianity. The idea that God is queer is only shocking because we already believe God isn't.

But if we think of God as queer in the context of sexual violence, we can think of God as at odds with the norms of gender, sexuality, and violence. These norms allow some people power over others based on gender and sexuality. The norms of homophobia and transphobia insist that LGBTQ people are sinners, deserving of God's punishment. To some, this means they are deserving of violence. Even people who do not engage in physical violence can participate in structural violence by supporting laws and policies that exclude LGBTQ people, discriminating against LGBTQ people, sending LGBTQ people to conversion therapy, or trying to exorcise LGBTQ demons and insisting they "pray the gay away."

Susan: I was a little late to the party. I didn't even begin to think to myself that I could be anything but straight until I was in my mid-twenties. Even as I began to have relationships with women, I told myself that I was really straight. "I just loved her." I'd grown up hearing an unequivocal condemnation of queer folks to hell, but at seminary I'd found other ways to read the few passages that even spoke to diverse sexual behaviors. Still, despite my intellectual embrace of LGBTQ identities, I felt deep shame about myself. Eventually, an out and proud partner helped me with that, but the cost of coming out was high. I was teaching at small Christian colleges as I began to struggle to understand my sexuality. These were not places that welcomed such a struggle, and so I had to keep quiet and hide who I was becoming. That sort of double life is emotionally and spiritually—and for some physically— death-dealing. I feared losing my job. I feared being shamed publicly. I feared the students, colleagues, and administrators who might find me out. Most of all, I feared not being true to myself. Eventually, I could no longer live like that, and so I left my teaching job with nothing else lined up, afraid I might never teach again. But I was free, and freedom was worth that terrible cost. Within a year, I found my place at Oregon State University in women studies, but I know this story doesn't always have a happy ending for everyone. I was fortunate. I survived those years caught in the grip of homophobic Christianity. Not everyone does.

The church has enacted terrible sexual violence on LGBTQ people. The Catholic Church has called queer people "inherently disordered." Conservative churches have railed against homosexuality and transgender identities. They have thrown LGBTQ people out of their congregations and told them they are going to hell. Mainline churches have fought over and sometimes split over acceptance of LGBTQ people in the church and as its ministers. Many denominations still refuse to ordain LGBTQ people even though they feel called by God to serve in that capacity. Churches have tried to force queer people to change their sexual identities, through spiritual and psychological (and sometimes physical) violence. Many Christians have supported laws to force trans people to use restrooms based on the gender identity that was assigned to them at birth rather than their actual gender identities. All of this increases risk for physical violence and death for LGBTQ people.

If these are the norms, the Queer God is the God who disrupts norms, who accepts LGBTQ people unconditionally, who celebrates LGBTQ identities, and who demands justice for LGBTQ people. Queer Asian American theologian Patrick Cheng suggests that God is Radical Love.[15] Radical Love, Cheng explains, dissolves barriers between the human and the divine, just as LGBTQ people dissolve barriers of gender and sexuality. Cheng also reminds us that sexuality and gender cannot be separated from race, class, ability, and other forms of difference. We must also dissolve the barriers between our analyses of sexism, racism, heterosexism, classism, and other systems of oppression.

Since the Queer God arises from the experiences of people marginalized because of their sexualities and genders, the Queer God offers a unique kind of hope and healing for people violated by sexual violence. Sexual violence and homophobia are two of the primary tools patriarchy uses to maintain itself. Sexual violence, which may be same-gender violence, rests on a framework of heteronormativity and patriarchy. Sexual violence is an assertion of male power and dominance, whether that dominance is over women, children, LGBTQ people, or other men. Sexual violence is a way of enacting masculinity, of claiming the privileged male position. Queerness challenges the very foundations of heteronormativity and patriarchy by rejecting fixed notions of gender and sexuality. This challenge opens up space to imagine a world without sexual violence.

The God Who Accompanies

Jo: The paradigm I really came to understand was church gives people three things: (i) a sense of worldview. It makes order out of chaos; (ii) a sense of community; and (iii) a sense of ritual. What I found is I could create those things without church and without spirituality. I found a sense of worldview in existential philosophy. I started reading existential philosophers and I really love Victor Frankl. Just this idea that life is meaningless and we have the responsibility to create meaning for ourselves. And that really help me to break the authoritarian image of "God is in control. I am not." It gave me total agency. And then God is an accompaniment or love is an accompaniment to your process.

I started playing with imagery. At first God became a source of just color. It didn't need to be a figure. It could be like a periwinkle, sparkly color. And it would surround me and just make me feel so loved and so supported and so held. And now I don't know.

It's like a state of being. I don't know that it has an image for me anymore as much as it's like there's been this presence accompanying me through life, and that presence doesn't need a form. It's a bit shapeless—which is maybe what love is—but I recognize it when it's nearby, or I call on it when I need it. It feels a bit more nebulous to me but no less no less constant.

Many people who experience sexual abuse eventually reject any idea of a God who resembles the God of their church or religious group. The notion of a personal God at all may be uncomfortable, tied as it is to traditional Christian faith. Surviving abuse may require leaving behind everything connected to the abuse, including a God who caused it, allowed it, or even witnessed it from afar. Abuse may shatter the possibility of a divine being. That doesn't mean people rule out Mystery or Presence in their lives, but, as Jo says, the notion of the divine becomes more nebulous. God is the Presence who accompanies them, even in a shapeless, nameless, unspeakable sort of way.

Other people may also experience God as accompaniment in a much more personal and relational way. This way of thinking about God allows us to feel God's presence, to recognize God accompanied us through our abuse and accompanies us still through our healing and thriving. The God Who Accompanies does not control but walks with us through whatever circumstances we face. This means we never face any aspect of our struggles or victories alone. Instead, we are always encircled by God's presence, whether as divine being or sparkly color. God is the Mystery within whom we live, and move, and have our being.

The God Who Overcomes (Even Trolls)

Susan: In the summer of 2020, wildfires raged only about 50 miles from my home in Oregon. I awoke one morning to a bright orange sky and dangerous air quality. Climate change and badly managed forests meant that the Willamette National Forest was very dry and full of fuel. About that same time, a new survey came out that showed white Christians are less likely to accept climate science than Christians of color or people of other religious faiths or no religious faith. So I wrote a piece for Baptist News Global arguing that the white supremacy underlying much of Christian faith has contributed to the vulnerability of poor people of color around the globe to the effects of climate change. First Campus Reform, a rightwing organization that uses students as reporters to "expose" liberal professors, and then Breitbart picked up on the essay and reported it as "Oregon professor says white Christians cause climate change." For the next five days my inbox was filled with vile, hateful, misogynistic, and homophobic email rants. My university administrators received emails suggesting the university get rid of me. Even the Oregon state senators received an email criticizing state funding being spent on professors like me.

I didn't know how bad things were going to get or how long the trolling would last. I was fortunate that my university supported me, and the trolling only lasted about five days. While the experience was horrible in many ways, it was also an amazing experience of grace. First, throughout it all, I felt an invisible barrier between me and the vile words the trolls sent. They didn't hurt my feelings or make me question myself. I'm not even sure what the trolls thought calling me names would accomplish. The experience was anxiety-provoking and exhausting but not devastating.

More importantly, the experience of grace came in the form of an outpouring of love and support. I heard from many more people offering kind words than from trolls. People I hadn't spoken to in decades got in touch to encourage me. Former students sent messages of concern. In fact, one of my former students is an Oregon state senator, and she responded to that email to the Senate with one of the most beautiful defenses of me I could have imagined.

The experience reminded me of the biblical story of Joseph, whose brothers had thrown him into a pit and then sold him into slavery in Egypt. Joseph eventually became a favorite of the pharaoh and rose to great prominence in Egypt. When a famine struck, Joseph's brothers showed up to ask for the help of the pharaoh, not knowing their brother was now in the pharaoh's court. When Joseph showed himself, they were terrified, but then Joseph said, "Even though you intended to do harm to me, God intended it for good." That's how I felt. Even though the trolls intended to do me harm, they actually gave me the most affirming day of my career with all of the love and care I was shown by so very many people! Not that I think God intended any of this—I'm a bit more like the Apostle Paul in thinking that God is at work in everything for good—not causing or controlling things but calling out the best in us, comforting, empowering, loving.

The God Who Overcomes is the One who is at work in the world, calling us to be the kind of people who live out God's love and justice. The God Who Overcomes helps us rebuild our lives following abuse and find wholeness, despite the remaining scars. We must recognize, however, that not everyone survives, not everyone overcomes. The consequences of sexual violence are deep and profound. Many die at the hands of abusers; others never return fully from the shattering that happens in violation. In the end, the God Who Overcomes embraces them, and all of us, at our last breath.

Susan: Grace and I disagree on what happens after we die. As a process thinker, I am open to novelty and so do make room for conscious awareness after death, but I don't expect it. I believe at death the entirety of our beings returns to the universe. I don't find despair in that, though; I find comfort. The atoms that make up my being, the particles that have existed in many forms since the Big Bang, return to the earth to nurture new life and become other things. For me, that's immortality enough. Everything that is resides in the Being of God, and so at death this body simply transforms into other forms within God's Being. I believe that, whatever happens at the moment of death, even and maybe especially a violent death—the end of conscious awareness or transition into an afterlife—we are fully embraced in the love of God, and so with God we overcome all our pain and suffering. Annie

Dillard says that she thinks that at the end our prayer is not "please" but "thank you."

Grace: I believe that there is an afterlife after death. Presbyterians talk about being in the immediate presence of God when we die. Life does not just end when we die on earth, but we come to the full glory of God's presence. As human beings, we are body and spirit. As our body perishes, our spirit lives on. The spirit unites with our creator, our God. We live forever in the presence of God. I don't know how this all happens as we are finite creatures and cannot comprehend the fullness of God and God's plans for us on earth and after we die. We live in faith that we will live after we perish on earth.

This assurance gives hope for us. Our lives are broken in so many ways. In times of difficulty and in experiences of sexual violence, we may want to die or not carry on anymore. During these moments of despair, we cling to the hope of life hereafter that God has promised to us.

In light of survivors' experiences of sexual violence, the time has come to abandon the Damaged God of traditional Christian thinking. Instead, survivors offer visions of a God who is with us through suffering and who calls for an end to suffering. The God of survivors calls for justice and for a transformation of society so that all people are valued and all of their needs are met, including the need for safety. Images of God drawn from survivors' experiences help us think about God as intimate, loving, supporting, and empowering. These images challenge notions of God as all-powerful, vengeful, and violent. Instead, they invite us into deeper communion with God and with one another. They remind us that violence is never God's way, nor should it be ours.

CHAPTER 6

Biblical Survivors in the First Testament

Susan: Looking back now, the disconnect surprises me. How could I not have seen the battered and broken bodies of women that litter the pages of Scripture? After all, I read the Bible through from cover to cover, Genesis to Revelation, every year from the time I was twelve years old until I was in my early twenties. Still, somehow my own abuse was never a lens through which I saw these women. I read and judged them as I had been taught to do as a fundamentalist Southern Baptist reader of the Bible. They were sinners, like Eve or the woman taken in adultery. Or they were merely props to move the story of God and God's men along, like Hagar or Jephthah's daughter. Their abuse, like mine, was unspoken, unconsidered, unimportant in the bigger story of an omnipotent God whose will was irresistible and unmovable. Their stories were of no comfort or use to me because I could not see myself in them. They were not the heroes of stories; they were objects of scorn or ridicule or pity; they were cautionary tales. That they could somehow speak to my anguish never occurred to me. As far as I could tell, the Bible had little to offer that addressed the wretchedness of my situation. I put the two things in separate boxes, and I stowed my abuse in the farthest corner of my mind, well away from Sunday school Bible studies and daily Bible readings.

Grace: My mother told me that the Bible was the written word of God and everything in it was the truth. The Bible was the holy word of God and sacred. We would not dare put another book or anything else on top of the Bible as it was sacrilegious to do so. Thus, it was with high reverence that we touched the Bible and read the Bible. When I was a child, my father ordered me the Picture Bible, *which was in three volumes. We were very poor, and my parents couldn't afford to buy books for us. My parents thought that if we needed books, we could borrow them at the school library. So, when the* Picture Bible *arrived, I read it from cover to cover many times. It had colorful drawings and easy-to-read comic strips. There were violent pictures and descriptions of war in Old Testament passages and disturbing admonishments in the New Testament about women being silent, and none of these verses ever bothered me. I just took it as the word of God, and I was to obey these words and live by these words as it was the living truth for my life.*

As I read the violent passages against women, such as Hagar, Lot's daughters, Levite's Concubine, Bathsheba, Esther, Vashti, and the woman caught in adultery, I didn't think twice about the violence or the inequality of women in these passages. I was not taught to question the violence or that patriarchy had allowed such violence to happen to these biblical women as well as the countless unmentioned women throughout biblical history. It was when I had to deal with my own abuse that I came to question some of the violence which existed in the pages of Scripture. Once I began questioning this sexual gendered violence, the questioning never stopped.

In this chapter, we aim to reclaim these stories, to read the "sad stories" of these "texts of terror," as feminist literary critic Phyllis Trible calls them.[1] By reading these stories with an intersectional feminist viewpoint, we sit in memoriam for these women; we identify with them and with all who suffer oppression and fight for justice.

These are the stories of women and others who suffer at the hands of men or an all-powerful God. Too many interpreters gloss over these stories of gender-based violence, refusing to see how prominent biblical men and a violent God are implicated in them. Instead, we approach these stories as Christian Testament scholar Elisabeth Schüssler Fiorenza suggests, with a "hermeneutics [interpretation] of suspicion" and a "hermeneutics of remembrance."[2] A hermeneutics of suspicion asks us to pay attention to how these stories have served patriarchy. Rather than simply taking these stories at face value, we must ask the question of who benefits from the telling of these stories in the ways we find them in the Bible. A hermeneutics of remembrance, on the other hand, allows us to reclaim past suffering as a "dangerous memory" that invites solidarity with those who struggle for justice.

As feminist readers of the Bible, we draw on traditional tools of biblical interpretation, looking at questions of who wrote the texts, who the intended audiences were, what language(s) were used in writing them, what type of writing the texts were intended to be, and what the themes of the texts were. We also bring a gender lens to our reading of the Bible. That means we pay attention to how texts were shaped by and shape patriarchy, how texts were used to harm women, and how women found empowerment in the Bible. We move women and marginalized others to the center of our interpretation, and we examine what biblical texts say and what they don't say about women.

We read "against the grain," refusing to accept traditional readings that have been done from men's perspectives and that serve men's interests. We question structures of power and seek liberatory readings of the texts. We engage perspectives of people who are different from ourselves to create kaleidoscopic readings of the texts, recognizing that diverse people enrich our readings with diverse perspectives, which we can hold together in tension simultaneously. Rather than looking for the "one right" interpretation, we open ourselves to multiple, even competing, interpretations that expand our possibilities for making sense of the texts. The readings of biblical survivors that we offer here start not with the texts or with traditional interpretive tools; rather they start with the experiences of diverse survivors who allow us to understand these biblical survivors in new and sometimes disconcerting ways. These readings, like the woman who will not allow the judge to rest, call out for justice.

Biblical critic Rhiannon Graybill reminds us that biblical stories of sexual violence create their own particular complications. She says these biblical passages in particular are "fuzzy, messy, icky." Fuzzy stories are those where the lines are not so clear, situations between clear consent and clear rape or sexual coercion. Messy stories defy "a tidy resolution." These stories often don't fit into familiar narratives of victimhood, suffering, and survival. The details are often messy, and the victim can be too, both psychologically and physically. Icky stories are about creepiness, shamefulness, grossness, and the complicated questions of power.[3] "Fuzzy, messy, icky" means we must read the biblical stories of sexual violence with openness to discomfort, ambivalence, and doubt, open to multiple perspectives and competing possibilities. We may not find a straight line from violence to redemption or from misogyny to liberation in these stories, and they may raise more questions than they answer.

The First Testament and Women

The Israelite family was a male-headed household, and property was inherited through men. Women were simply aliens or transients within their family of residence. Women's realm was in the home, and men's was in the public. Even today, in Korea wives are called *anae*, which literally means "inside person." A woman is someone who remains in the household quarters and does not roam outside the household. During the times of the First Testament,[4] men had legal authority over women in the family, and Israelite women's legal status was subordinate to that of men. Certainly, women were part of the community that the First Testament addresses, but the Law only speaks directly to men. Women are not addressed explicitly as women but are subsumed under husbands or male heads of households.[5]

In the First Testament, women are counted among men's possessions, along with children, slaves, and livestock (e.g., Exodus 20:17; Deuteronomy 5:21). While the First Testament outlines some rights for women—a wife's right to maintenance, a daughter's right to inheritance in the absence of sons, and the right of daughters, wives, and unattached women to make binding religious vows—it still overwhelmingly presents women as subordinate to and the property of men.[6] Because women are property, rape is not a crime against women but rather against the men to whom the women belong. Rape of men by men is an act of humiliation by forcing men into the role of women. Rape of women is also an act to humiliate men because it implies men cannot protect their women, their property, and again calls their masculinity into question.

Most of the women who show up in the Bible are unnamed. In fact, under 10 percent of the Bible's named characters are women. Women are also usually not in the forefront of public life in the Bible, and women who are named are usually prominent for unusual reasons; they are in some way "exceptional" women.

One common literary device that signals these named and exceptional women is "reversal." In a reversal, a woman overturns human power structures. For example, when Nabal refuses to share his wealth with David, David sets out to kill him and all the men in his family (I Samuel 25). Nabal's wife Abigail hears about David's plan and sets out to meet him with food and gifts. She throws herself at David's feet, flatters him, and convinces him that by sparing Nabal and his men David is avoiding the sin of bloodguilt. David agrees and commends her for her "good sense." The story then takes a troubling turn when we find out that, a few days later, God strikes Nabal dead, and so David decides to take Abigail as his wife. The text tells us that Abigail agreed, but we do have to ask how much choice she really would have had to say no to David. So while Abigail subverts power by outsmarting her husband and manipulating David, the text quickly puts her back in her place with her subordination to David as his wife.

Another example of reversal comes from the story of Jael, a Kenite woman (Judges 4–5). Deborah sends her army to do battle with the army of Canaanite king Jaban. When the Israelite army begins to win the battle, Jaban's commander Sisera flees and hides in the tent of Jael, asking her to keep watch while he sleeps and to lie if anyone asks if there's anyone else in the tent. She agrees, and then, when Sisera falls asleep, she drives a tent peg through his head and kills him, again turning power upside down.

While we find these exceptional women throughout the First Testament, we most often find women in their place—submissive, silent, invisible. The biblical text also often puts women in their place, blaming them for their sexuality, punishing them for stepping outside traditional expectations for womanhood, and enforcing their subordinate status through sexual assault and rape. These stories of sexual violence are fuzzy and icky—and yet we find that as we apply intersectional feminist lenses to reading these stories we create possibilities for surviving and thriving, even as we take seriously the violation and trauma of sexual violence.

Eve

The story of Eve may seem a surprising place to start our exploration of biblical survivors. After all, we don't think of Eve as a victim of sexual abuse or assault. And yet, in millennia of interpretations of Eve's story, we find a religious justification for women's subordination, compulsory heterosexuality (the enforcement of heterosexuality onto all people), and sexual shaming/blaming of women. While the biblical text of Eve's story is not one of sexual abuse, the history of its interpretation certainly is one. Patriarchal interpreters turn Eve into a sexual temptress, the source of evil in the world, the origin of women's pain in childbirth and subordination to men, and the reason for sexual shame and the need for men's control of women's sexuality.

Feminist biblical scholars point out that neither story of creation in Genesis 1 or 2 assumes or mandates women's subordination. In fact, these stories depict a rather egalitarian relationship in the Garden of Eden. Only through the Fall does patriarchal dominance become a feature of human relationships; God does not issue male dominance as a punishment. Rather, dominance begins because the actions of the story rupture trust and rupture the egalitarian relationship between the woman and man that God had intended.[7]

Within patriarchy, then, the subordinate role of Eve is placed on all women thereafter. Many later interpreters view Eve as the one responsible for bringing sin and death into the world. She is the one who "tempted" Adam to eat of the fruit of the tree of the knowledge of good and evil. Along the way, Eve's temptation of Adam also takes on a sexual association, and all women are painted as sexual temptresses who must be controlled.

Within this framework, Eve becomes a victim of sexual shaming. While the text tells us that both the woman and the man are ashamed before one another and before God, subsequent patriarchal interpretations have turned this shared shame into sexual shaming of Eve alone. The text itself does not make subordination and painful childbearing a punishment for eating the fruit. The punishment is expulsion from the garden. The consequences of expulsion are what the author sees in the world around him—toil in the fields, painful childbirth, and domination of men over women. These are not God's intention for humans, nor God's punishment for them. Rather, they are a description of the world as it exists. In fact, the word translated as "pain" is actually the word "toil," which elsewhere in the text simply means human labor. Yet, this translation has meant many women through the ages have seen sexual shame and the pain of childbirth as deserved experiences because of the Fall.[8]

Lesbian feminist biblical scholar Deryn Guest suggests that presenting gender complementarity (having different roles based on gender) and hierarchy as God-ordained is a strategy to suppress women.[9] She also argues that the story of Eve reinforces heterosexual norms. Read from a lesbian feminist perspective, however, the story may tell us how women's sexual drive had to be directed specifically toward men or may (with a bit of humor) point out that the woman's desire for her husband is included in the punishments for eating the fruit. Guest asks why the woman's sexual desire has to be directed toward the man. She wonders if women have so little to gain from the system of complementarity that they just might walk away from it if they aren't convinced it's God-ordained.[10] Perhaps the text is hinting that women's desire might be directed elsewhere if it isn't controlled by religion and men.

The Midrash is a collection of creative Jewish interpretations by rabbis that was compiled from around the fourth to the twelfth century. Many Christians don't know this tradition, but it tells us that the first woman who is created in the first creation story is Lilith. Lilith sees herself as Adam's equal and refuses sex laying beneath Adam. Eventually Adam tries to force Lilith, and Lilith leaves the garden. God sends angels to try to convince her to come back, but she refuses to return to a subordinate relationship. According to the stories, she then has sexual relationships with demons and bears demon children. She becomes a danger to infants and men because of her rage and sexual seduction. Some interpreters even suggest she is the serpent in the garden. God then has to create another partner for Adam, and this story, told in the second creation account, is the story of Eve, a woman who is willing to submit to Adam.

Many feminists have embraced Lilith as a feminist icon. Unlike Eve, Lilith is strong and independent. She demands equality, and, when Adam uses violence to try to dominate her, she leaves and becomes a terror to patriarchal society.

For survivors, both the stories of Eve and Lilith can serve as empowering tales. Certainly, we recognize that there are a lot of competing interpretations—some justify women's subordination, and some advance equality and justice for women. When we read the Bible for liberation, we look for readings that move us toward freedom and critique readings that harm, disempower, and oppress people. In other words, we judge a text, not by what it says, but by what it does. Does it move us toward liberation or toward subjugation? This means we can decidedly reject readings of Eve's story that promote women's subordination and embrace readings that affirm equality as God's intention. We can also turn to Lilith as a figure who challenges traditional readings of the creation stories and offers an alternative to submission and subordination.

Lot's Daughters

For survivors of incest, this may be the ickiest passage of them all. This story follows the destruction of Sodom and the death of Lot's wife. Lot and his daughters end up in a cave—and in the First Testament, nothing good ever happens in a cave.[11] The story tells us that, believing they are the only people left in the world, the daughters conspire to get Lot drunk and have sex with him so they'll get pregnant and continue the human race. The sons they bear become the fathers of nations that are enemies of Israel: Moab and Ammon.

Some feminist interpreters read this as a story of the daughters taking power back from Lot, who had earlier offered them up for gang rape to a mob of men at his door. However, we're not sure that sexual violence in response to sexual violence is really an empowering way to read this passage. Other interpreters argue that Lot is actually the one who victimized his daughters, but the story turns the situation around as a way to exonerate Lot. Biblical scholar Irmtraud Fischer says this reading of the text imagines it as a "hushed-up story of incest,"[12] as so many of them are.

Biblical scholar Wil Gafney points out that Lot comes from an incestuous family. Sarah and Abraham are sister and brother. One of Abraham's nieces, Lot's sister, marries another of Abraham's brothers, her uncle. Gafney thinks the acceptance of incest within Lot's family may play a role in his relationship with his daughters. At the time, such relationships were not forbidden and may have been part of the local culture.[13] That still does nothing to lessen the ickiness for most modern readers!

As Rhiannon Graybill notes, whatever really happens in the story, it's still about sexual transgression.[14] It's icky because it violates the incest taboo, involves excessive drinking, and results in pregnancies that lead to generations of warfare. By the time the Israelite Elimelech and his wife, Naomi, move to Moab to escape famine, Israelites have long considered Moabites to be degenerate and thought Moabite women to be instruments of impurity and evil. In fact, Deuteronomy tells us that to the tenth generation "no Ammonite or Moabite shall be admitted to the assembly of the Lord" (23:3). That's an awfully long time to hold a grudge! One commentator says this story is really about telling readers that Moabites and Ammonites are "incestuous bastards."[15] This belief justifies David's massacre of Moabites (II Samuel 8:2) and plundering of Ammonites (II Samuel 12:26–31). In fact, Cherokee literary scholar Laura Donaldson reads this narrative from the perspective of Indigenous women in the Americas who, like the Moabite women, were hypersexualized as the Other.[16]

Nonetheless, Graybill says we should "stay with the trouble."[17] By that, she means that we have to keep engaging with the story in all its ickiness. We sit with its complexities and ambiguities and troubling, troubling possibilities. She adds that, rather than glossing over these problems in the story, we can do a "reparative reading." Reparative reading, she says, "does not dismiss the pain of these stories but instead opens the possibility of imagining an *after* to such pain. . . . Reparative reading . . . suggests that we can imagine an *after* to sexual trauma in the Bible without erasing that trauma itself."[18] Graybill reminds us that, for most of us, life goes on after trauma and that we can imagine a life after trauma.

Dinah

Dinah's story in Genesis 34 is another icky, messy story. Dinah is the seventh child and the only daughter of Leah and Jacob. Dinah sets out to seek companionship with other women in the region, and, along the way, a prince named Shechem rapes her. In First Testament times, a woman's virginity was crucial to a father's ability to marry her off. If a woman were not a virgin, a father could never collect the full bride price or could be burdened with supporting his daughter for life. Marriage was essentially a monetary exchange between men, and a woman's virginity was a crucial part of these negotiations. If a virgin had sex out of wedlock—whether seduced or raped— she became devalued and brought shame upon the family. If it became known publicly that Dinah had been raped, it would bring insult to Jacob's honor and to the honor of the men in her family. When Shechem rapes Dinah, he not only insults the men of the family, he essentially makes Dinah damaged goods that will no longer bring a full price.

In the First Testament, as we will continue to see, women are most often objects in transactions between men. In Dinah's case, she herself never speaks and eventually disappears from her own story, which becomes the story of the men in her family. Essentially, Dinah, like so many of these biblical women, is trafficked, traded to Shechem as part of a plot to restore the honor of her family, whose property has been devalued by her rape. We'll return to this theme of trafficking in the stories of Esther and David's women, where we'll find even God implicated in the trading of women as sexual objects.

Dinah's story, like those of other biblical women, also lends itself to diverse readings. In fact, a tradition from the Midrash offers interesting possibilities for a queer reading of Dinah's story. One tradition in the Midrash holds that Leah's seventh child was originally a male fetus in her womb, but Rachel prayed for the fetus's sex to change. Another tradition says that Leah herself prayed to change the fetus's sex so that Rachel might have a son to be the father of one of the twelve tribes of Israel.

This tradition suggests ways we can offer a queer reading of Dinah's story, with Dinah as a transgender or queer character whose independence is punished because she steps outside the constraints of gender, sexuality, and traditional womanhood. The Bible tells us that Dinah went out to visit the women of the region. In this act, Dinah asserts her independence and goes out in search of the companionship of other women. Instead, the story crushes her desire for autonomy and the company of women by subjecting her to rape by Shechem. Feminist biblical scholar Susana Scholz suggests the rest of the story is not about Shechem's love for Dinah but his continued desire to dominate her. She translates the word for love as "lust" or "desire," which is about "Shechem's intention . . . to treat Dinah as he pleases." Rather than speaking tenderly in a romantic way to Dinah, Shechem attempts to "soothe the young woman" who is upset by her assault.[19] Then his request to have her for marriage becomes a transaction between men in which Dinah has no say, as in the rape itself.

A postcolonial reading of the story adds another element, recognizing Dinah's story as a justification for possession of someone else's land. Already, as African feminist Musa Dube tells us, we know that Dinah's father is a colonizer, and Shechem's rape of Dinah and her subsequent devaluation give Jacob and his sons further reason to take Canaanites' land.[20] The story then becomes one that furthers the interests of the colonizer.

Jacob is silent about the marriage request, but Dinah's brothers are distressed. They are upset that their sister is no longer a virgin. As a result, the brothers devise a plan and demand Shechem and all the men of the town circumcise themselves before intermarrying with Jacob's family. They agree to do so, but, on the third day, when all the men are in dire pain from the circumcision, Simeon and Levi (brothers of Dinah) slaughter all the men and rescue Dinah from Shechem's house (v. 26). The other brothers then loot the town in revenge for defiling and dishonoring their sister (v. 27). Jacob isn't happy about these actions, but the brothers say, "should our sister be treated like whore?" (34:31).[21]

This story erases Dinah's personhood and agency as she does not speak and acts only once (34:1), after which she is referred to as an object and never as a subject. After the brothers arrive, she is only mentioned by name once between verses 6 and 25 and appears again only in the genealogy in Genesis 45:15. Rosemary Radford Ruether reminds us that in patriarchal theology the male is the normative and dominant representative of the human species and becomes the norm for imagining God, for defining sin, redemption, and ministry. The female is seen as subordinate and auxiliary to the male. Therefore, women never appear in patriarchal theology as representatives of humanity as such. Their normative position is that of absence and silence. When patriarchal theology mentions women, it does so to reinforce its definition of their "place" in its system.[22] We need to remember this in the story of Dinah as she is subordinate and auxiliary to the men, which reinforces the sexual violence committed against her will. As a violated young woman, she becomes a pawn among her brothers, her father, and the man who committed violence against her. She disappears from her own story, which becomes fully a story of transactions between men and the right to colonize another's land. We never know what Dinah wants.

Jo: I was raised Opus Dei Catholic. Self-mortification was the way to salvation in Opus Dei theology. It was about being in pain and aligning with the suffering of Christ so that you could be saved. And my family ran with that. It was like men are the crosses that you carry. They have no responsibility and you have to, as a woman or as a child, bear the burden of their dysfunction, their bodies, their power abuses. That is the cross that you carry. So, there was always a justification of suffering as opposed to a liberation from it. Unfortunately, I got in a fight with one of my brothers once and he wrote it all down and emailed it to me, because we weren't speaking in person. He literally said to me, "Love requires that you stay in an abusive relationship." Like that is what God wants. He literally said that. And that feels so crazy if you weren't raised in that environment, but when you're raised by a narcissist who claims he's God and uses this tradition of mortification and suffering that is grounded in history, and then that human is married to a codependent other human who is constantly justifying and enabling his violence, you get ideologically trapped. And I feel so lucky that I was so well educated and so drawn to liberation because I got out, but I feel so deeply sad because I'm the only one in my family that has left, and all of us were sexually abused. I don't have evidence it was everyone, but I have a lot of cousins, and a lot of them came forward when I did and they're like, "We just have to forgive. This is what God wants—the family to stay together." So, there is a strong theological narrative of manipulation. That is not God at all, that is not love at all. But it's certainly what my family teaches in order to keep women and children in the hands of violence and that violence passing down through generations.

A resistant feminist reading of Dinah's story returns her agency and makes her liaison with Shechem a consensual one. As we've mentioned before, women's consent as we understand it would have been a foreign concept in these times, but by framing the story as Dinah's choice, feminist readers can restore her personhood and autonomy. Anita Diamant's novel, *The Red Tent*, takes this perspective and centers the women in the story. In the novel, the story becomes a narrative of conflict between gender, nation, and class that challenges male structures of power.

The many and diverse readings of this story are needed to disrupt traditional readings that subordinate women. Diverse readings allow us to complicate Dinah's story in ways that can be useful for survivors. In critiquing the story, we name her rape as an act of violence, and we recognize the far-reaching consequences of her rape. We also recognize the harmful ways patriarchal structures constrain Dinah and eventually remove her from her own story. We find possibilities for reading Dinah's agency back into the story by imagining her as an autonomous woman-identified-woman or reimagining her encounter with Shechem as her own choice and giving her a full life beyond her disappearance from the biblical story. For survivors, Dinah's story both affirms the injustice of sexual abuse and suggests the importance of telling our own stories rather than disappearing from them. A feminist reading of Dinah recenters women, just as survivors should be the center of their own stories.

A survivor wrote:

Silent Secrets

My body pays the price
for my mouth's betrayal
But I will not keep locked away
those silent secrets
in the bowels of my memory.
My warring demon
will not silence me again.
I will scream
from the mountaintops
to spit you out
to expel you with the same force
with which you entered uninvited.
I will tell my story
and I will pay the price
that sets me free.
Sleepless night on the bathroom floor
may be my currency
for settling our old debt
But I will tell my story
and I will be free.

Hagar

Hagar is coerced.

Hagar is an enslaved Egyptian woman and a handmaiden of Sarai, the wife of Abram. God has promised Abram and Sarai a child, but Sarai is getting too old to bear children, so she takes matters into her own hands. Since Sarai is barren, she hopes to start a family through her handmaiden, Hagar. Sarai gives Hagar to Abram to rape so she can bear him a child, an heir.

What happens between Abram and Hagar is rape. As an enslaved woman, Hagar does not have power to consent to the arrangement made between Abram and Sarai. Too often the church has glossed over this fact in its focus on God's promise to Abram. We imagine, too, that most in the church would not like to think of Abram as a rapist and so explain the rape away as a function of the time. Just because people of that time had a different notion of consent than we do, does not make this story any less violent. If we imagine ourselves in Hagar's position, we don't think that any one of us would enjoy or willingly accept enslavement or coerced sex simply because it is characteristic of the time. Unwanted sex is and always has been wrong because it violates and denies the humanity of the victim. Just because enslavement allows Abraham sexual access to Hagar does not make it right.

In many ways, this story of sexual violence is a familiar one of male power, and yet it is complicated by the relationship between the two women in the story. Hagar is Sarai's slave; she gives her to Abram to be raped, and, in fact, the rape is her idea. This story of Hagar is difficult to read as it is about exploitation and persecution suffered by an enslaved woman, not only at the hands of a man but also at the hands of her mistress. It is a story of conflict with women betraying women and mothers conspiring against mothers. It is a story of social rivalry.[23]

This story also features important intersections of identity and power as central elements in the relationship between Hagar and Sarai. While both are women, Sarai is part of a higher social class, an owner of an enslaved woman. Hagar is also defined by ethnicity, an Egyptian, a foreigner. Yet all the social power does not reside with Sarai. Sarai is infertile; Hagar is the one who can bear children, and, in fact, the story tells us that this makes Hagar contemptuous of Sarai. We see, however, that the sexual violence of the first part of the story continues in another form in the second part of the story as Sarah mistreats Hagar, to the point that Hagar flees. Rhiannon Graybill focuses our attention on this story for its fuzziness, messiness, and ickiness in the relationship between these two women. She says the intimacy the two women share leads to disgust with one another.[24] And in many ways, this story really is much more about the relationship between the women than about Abram and his offspring.

A queer reading of the story also asks us to center this relationship between Hagar and Sarai and imagine the complexities involved. The text is clear that Hagar is Sarai's slave. What, we may ask, was their relationship before Sarai gave Hagar to Abram? What intimacies were shared between these women? How might Hagar have experienced Sarai's betrayal when she gave Hagar to Abram to be raped and then turned against her once she became pregnant? While in one way this is a story of heterosexual rape, it is also a story of women's relationships. Graybill says we should find ways to "talk about female relationships and sexual and other forms of violence together, without subordinating the former to the latter."[25]

Womanist (Black feminist) scholars read this story as the story of an enslaved African/Black woman. They connect stories of enslavement and Blackness with Hagar and with contemporary experiences of Black women.[26] This story is reminiscent of the accounts of enslaved African women and white enslavers during enslavement. There are countless stories of brutal rapes of Black women by their white enslavers, which were compounded by beatings by resentful white wives who penalized enslaved women for their own rapes. Enslaved women at times conceded to their white master's advances as a way to protect their family from being beaten and to prevent themselves and their families from being sold away. It also at times helped them elevate their social rank in order to protect themselves from vicious overseers.[27]

Alongside the story of betrayal, violence, rape, and jealousy, however, is a counternarrative. In this story, God comes to Hagar and meets her in the wilderness. Even this counternarrative is problematic because she's told to return to her enslavement and submit to Sarai. Her consolation is her son. Nonetheless, God does meet Hagar in the desert. This theophany—encounter with God—is highly unusual in the Bible because these encounters are given almost exclusively to men.[28] Still, Hagar becomes the first person to name the Lord who spoke to her: "You are El-roi," she says. "Have I really seen God and remained alive after seeing him?" (Genesis 16:13). The circumstance of Hagar's theophany is extraordinary and meaningful, especially within the patriarchal context of Scripture. It becomes a central focus of the counternarrative that uplifts all abused women of color, who, like Hagar, may encounter God.

For survivors, especially women of color, Hagar's story captures the complexities of sexual betrayal and rape within families. Often survivors face not only the betrayal of being sexually assaulted by a family member but also the betrayal of the women in the family who may enable abuse or take the side of the perpetrator. Similarly, victims of clergy abuse experience betrayal at the hands of trusted community members beyond their abuser, including other women in the faith community.

The comfort for survivors in this story is the counternarrative in which God comes to Hagar both times she is in the wilderness after fleeing Abraham and Sarah's home. In the second story, God intervenes and saves Hagar's son. Notably, this time God does not tell Hagar to return. From this story, survivors can claim encounter with God. For liberationists, this story shows God siding with the oppressed in Hagar in her liberation from Abraham and Sarah. Similarly, survivors can assert God's favor for them and their liberation from sexual violence.

Bathsheba

In the book of Samuel, Bathsheba, "daughter of Sheba," is the daughter of Eliam and probably of noble birth. Bathsheba is the wife of Uriah the Hittite. Biblical scholars note that the fact that Bathsheba is identified by her relationship with two men (when in all other instances women are identified by only one predominant male relationship) makes clear that she belongs to someone and is in absolutely no way available for David. Yet, David notices her and decides he has to have her anyway.

Many interpreters have made much of the beginning of the story, where we find Bathsheba bathing on her rooftop. Again, Bathsheba, like Eve, is labeled as a temptress, seeking to seduce David. While some interpreters use this possibility as a way to give Bathsheba agency and even suggest she is a cunning woman who used her sexuality to improve her lot in life, many interpreters uses this as a way to blame Bathsheba for what happens and exonerate David from responsibility, even to the point of making David the victim in the story.

David sends his men to take Bathsheba. Notice throughout the Bible how often that word is used to describe men's actions toward women.[29] They "take" them as if they are mere objects to be possessed. Even God is implicated in this taking, sometimes ordering men to "take" women as part of their conquest. When Nathan confronts David about his sin with Bathsheba, he gives David this message from God: "I will take your wives before your eyes, and give them to your neighbor, and he shall lie with your wives in the sight of this very sun" (II Samuel 12:11). Again, we see women as objects for transactions between men, including the male God of this text.

The Bible doesn't state whether Bathsheba consents to sex, but there is obviously a power differential, and it would have been impossible to disobey the king. We don't know what Bathsheba wants, but it doesn't really matter because she is what David wants. This lack of clarity about sexual violence is a key feature of this story.[30] Bathsheba has no agency and no power in this narrative. King David rapes Bathsheba, who could not have consented because of this huge power gap between her and an authoritative king.[31] After the rape, David sends her home, and soon thereafter she sends David a message: "I'm pregnant."

David knows that Bathsheba's pregnancy is the result of his act. Likely, what David saw earlier was Bathsheba taking part in a ritual of purification following her period. Since she has just had her period, there is no possibility that she is pregnant with Uriah's child because Uriah is off fighting a war. This leaves David with a big problem. How is he to cover his sin if Uriah is on the battlefield? So he knows he has to find a way to ensure Uriah will have sex with Bathsheba.[32] King David summons Uriah from the battlefield in the hope that Uriah will have sex with Bathsheba and think that the child belongs to him. Uriah, however, is unwilling to violate the ancient norms applying to warriors in active service. Rather than go home to his wife, he remains with the palace troops.

After several attempts to convince Uriah to sleep with Bathsheba, David gives the order to his general, Joab, that Uriah should be placed on the front lines of the battle, where Uriah will be more likely to be killed. David has Uriah carry the message that leads to his death. Again, this story becomes one where one violent action leads to another and eventually to two deaths.

After Uriah has been killed, David marries Bathsheba. Their first child dies as a divine punishment from God for David's adultery, sexual assault, and murder of Uriah. David repents and Bathsheba later has another child, Solomon. This part of the story is highly problematic, depicting God as willing to kill an infant to punish David. Like the book of Job, it also assumes a replacement child is the answer, as if new children somehow mitigate the unjust loss and grief of other children.

When David is old, Bathsheba and the prophet Nathan convince David to let Solomon take the throne instead of an older brother, Adonijah. As a result, Bathsheba becomes queen mother. Some interpreters suggest this is evidence of the success of Bathsheba's earlier plot to seduce David, and some read that as a way Bathsheba enacts agency, while others read it as a reflection of Bathsheba's temptation of David. We don't know. The text never tells us what Bathsheba wants. As in Dinah's story, the preponderance of evidence suggests Bathsheba's encounter with David is a rape, but the text is just vague enough to allow a reading that gives Bathsheba agency and choice in what happened.[33] We can hold both of these possibilities in mind at the same time to suggest various options for survivors to read the text in helpful ways

Many survivors can no doubt identify with Bathsheba as someone sexually assaulted by a man with institutional power over them—a teacher, a coach, a father, a priest, or a pastor. Many of us know the betrayal of being abused by someone we are supposed to be able to trust.

In addition, many sexual relationships have a similarly complex and messy context of consent. When men in power groom women and children for sexual abuse, they use their influence over those who are supposed to be under their care to create trust and dependence. They may even convince them that they desire a sexual relationship. Feminists have been clear: within relationships of unequal power, people with less power cannot consent because of the inherently coercive nature of the relationship. Some feminists do argue that this perspective takes agency away from adult women (never children), but agency always exists within constraints. Abused people still always have agency. That may not be the agency to say yes or no, but it is the agency to survive. Whether Bathsheba wants a sexual relationship with David or not, she enacts agency by surviving and then finding ways to access power in David's house. That's not necessarily a satisfactory resolution. After all, Bathsheba is married to her rapist (and keep in mind that Bathsheba is still only one of David's many concubines and wives, not a wife in a monogamous marriage as we think of them today), and the text gives her no say in that either.

Bathsheba's story also reminds us of the importance of what people want for themselves. People should be able to have their boundaries, trust those with power over them, and say what they want. This includes survivors, who should be the ones to say what they want for their own recoveries and healing. We don't know what Bathsheba wants, but we should be able to be clear about what we want.

Tamar

Unlike with Dinah and Bathsheba, we have no room for doubt about what happens to Tamar. Tamar is the daughter of King David and Maacah, who was the daughter of Talmai, the king of Geshur. Tamar is a sister of Absalom, and Amnon is her half-brother. 2 Samuel 13 records the story of Tamar, who is raped by Amnon. In the narrative, Amnon becomes obsessed with Tamar, who is said to be beautiful like her brother, Absalom. Amnon's friend and cousin Jonadab devises a plan in which Amnon pretends to be ill and asks Tamar to come to his room to prepare him some food. King David facilitates this ruse and hence becomes part of his daughter's violation (2 Samuel 13:1–22). King David sends Tamar to Amnon's house, and Amnon watches her while she prepares the food. When she brings it to him, he presses her for sex. To his advances, Tamar responds, "No, my brother, do not force me; for such a thing is not done in Israel; do not do anything so vile!" (2 Samuel 13:11–12). Despite her vehement refusal, he rapes her.

After the rape, Amnon treats Tamar disdainfully and sends her home, hating her more than he had loved her. Desolate, Tamar tears her robe and marks her forehead with ashes. She goes to her brother Absalom, who is unable to comfort her. When King David hears of her rape, he's angry but does nothing about it. Two years later, Absalom takes his revenge by having Amnon murdered.

In *The Cry of Tamar: Violence against Women and the Church's Response*, Episcopal priest Pamela Cooper-White writes that Tamar's story is a message of violence against women for the church.[34] The story of Tamar's rape is told from a man's perspective with an emphasis on the male roles in the story: David, Amnon, and Absalom. "Even the poignancy of Tamar's humiliation is drawn out for the primary purpose of justifying Absalom's later murder of Amnon, and not for its own sake."[35] Again, a violated woman becomes a secondary character in the story of her rape.

Phyllis Trible highlights the patterns of power struggle between the men and the vulnerability of Tamar, the sole woman in the narrative. Trible argues that when Tamar is finally given a voice (she is speechless for the first eleven verses of the narrative), "the narrator hints at her powerlessness by avoiding her name."[36] The words of Jonadab, Amnon, Absalom, and David are consistently introduced by the proper name of each. The first time Tamar speaks, however, the narrator prefaces it using the pronoun "she." This illustrates the lack of agency and power that Tamar and other women have. Trible says that "this subtle difference suggests the plight of the female."[37]

Trible points out Tamar's wisdom and eye for justice. She points to Tamar's request that Amnon simply "speak to the king, for he will not keep (Tamar) from (Amnon)" (13:13). In other words, Tamar recognizes that David will give her to Amnon if he asks. Again, we don't know if this is what Tamar wants, but Trible argues that "her words are honest and poignant; they acknowledge female servitude."[38] Tamar is wise and understands her place in the world and is willing to work within it. Even after Amnon violently rapes her, she pleads for justice, not letting anger cloud her judgment.[39] Rhiannon Graybill suggests, rather, that Tamar shrewdly looks out for her own interests.[40] While as modern readers we would not want Tamar to marry her rapist, for her in the culture of the time that may have seemed her best option. Her rape would have made her damaged goods and likely ended her prospects for marriage, leaving her only with the option of remaining in her father's house for life. Perhaps, for reasons all her own, life with Amnon feels a better alternative than life in David's house.

As before, sexual violation is a justification for more violence. Tamar's brother Absalom has Amnon killed. While the Bible tells us this is because Absalom hates Amnon for raping Tamar, the act also conveniently removes Absalom's competition for the throne. This reading of the story is reinforced later when Absalom asserts his place as king by publicly having sex with David's concubines. His sexual conquest reflects his conquest of David's throne, and again we see women as the bargaining chips in men's transactions. Neither do we imagine these women give their consent. No one in the text seems to have any concern for them, and, while David is inconsolable over the death of Absalom, he simply secludes these women who are now damaged goods for the rest of their lives.[41]

In Tamar's story, we see women again used as currency between men, and we see Tamar negotiating as best she can, given the constraints of her context. Many survivors can identify with Tamar's clear "No!" and the willingness of perpetrators to ignore what victims want and even use brute force to exert sexual power. Like Tamar, many survivors are still willing to work within the very contexts that limit and harm them, and, like Tamar, they discover the extent to which patriarchal contexts violate, silence, and damage them.

Vashti and Esther

About half of sexual assaults in the United States involve alcohol. The stories of Vashti and Esther are no different in that way. Their stories begin with a party given by the king for his men friends. One biblical scholar even translates the word the NRSV renders as "banquet" as a "drinking party."[42] The king has been drinking—a lot. The KJV tells us that, on the seventh day, "the heart of the king was merry with wine." In Hebrew culture at the time, however, the heart was considered the seat of thought, so the passage is really telling us that the wine has gone to the king's head.[43] He's drunk.

In his drunken state, the king decides he wants to trot his queen, Vashti, out in front of all of his friends. After all, he has already been flaunting his great wealth and power. Why not also show off his beautiful wife as one more way to exert his power over the other men in the kingdom? So, he commands seven eunuchs to go and get the queen and bring her to the party, wearing the crown. The king's use of the word "bring" shows how he sees Vashti as an object, another possession among the many he has already been showing off to his friends. His later reaction to Vashti's refusal underlines what he had in mind. He asks what's to be done to Vashti for not *performing* his command.[44]

The eunuchs find the queen and convey the king's command. Queen Vashti, however, is hosting her own party for women. She likely realizes that she will be the only woman in a roomful of drunken men. Most significantly, many scholars read this text to say that the king has commanded Vashti to come before the group wearing *only* the crown. He wants her naked.

One scholar points out that the fact that the women are not in the presence of the king means they are not fully under his control. Exclusion, he explains, results in losing control over the person or group who is excluded.[45] Vashti says no.

The king is furious and consults with his advisors who blow the situation all out of proportion, arguing that Vashti's refusal will lead to women everywhere in the kingdom refusing their husbands' commands. So, Vashti is stripped of her title and banished from the king's presence.

Now the king must find a replacement, and his advisors suggest a beauty pageant.[46] As Elaine Heath points out, many have heard this story in Sunday school and thought of a contest with willing participants, much like the Miss America Pageant, with the prize being becoming a queen. That image, however, obscures the much bleaker reality. None of these girls really has a choice. They cannot say no. Like many girls around the world today, these girls are plucked from their families, groomed, and sent one by one to have sex with the king. After that, they are sent back to the harem to be one of the king's concubines, sexually available to him at his whim.

These girls are not unlike victims of sex trafficking today. Often traffickers target girls in communities made vulnerable by poverty, racism, and colonialism. They kidnap them or convince their parents to sell them or lie that they are taking the girls to good jobs in other countries. Reading Esther's story from their perspective highlights the dehumanization and commodification of the king's beauty pageant.

Dawn: At fifteen years old, I met my abuser/exploiter. My great-grandmother passed away feeling abandoned by God, my parents had divorced, and I had chosen to move to California under my father's supervision. My abuser targeted and groomed me quickly, while my father was more interested in getting high. My abuser scoffed at Christianity, made fun of his own mother for her evangelical rigidity, and I easily fell into his beliefs, having had my own experience of God as punishing and absent, who bestowed favors on everyone other than me. As my grooming turned into deeper and deeper psychological, emotional, sexual, and physical abuse, I saw God as more than just punishing, but as intentionally seeking to cause harm—a sadist. My core pain was overwhelming, and in my mind, there was no other explanation for God, if there really was one. My thoughts about God during these years were not only that "He" caused pain and trauma, but that there was no escape—no way to ever be out from "under His thumb."

We see too that Esther is doubly vulnerable, as are most trafficked girls. Today, most of the top sex tourism destinations are in the Global South, and most sex tourists are white Western men, often paying for sex with children and young teens. Esther replaces Vashti as queen, but she is still a young woman and a Jew, and that identity puts her at risk in a royal court where men compete for power, and perceived slights are considered political threats.

Haman, one of the king's top advisors, has it in for the Jews because Mordecai, Esther's uncle, will not bow down before him. Haman eventually incites the king to begin an ethnic cleansing.[47] At this moment, as queer interpreters note, Esther "comes out of the closet" as a Jew.[48] She uses her status as queen to change the king's mind and ensure the survival of her people. For many survivors, Esther's story is one of resistance and transformation. For others, however, it is yet another story of a young woman put in a position to sacrifice herself, sexually and mortally, for others. For them, Esther's uncle Mordecai's manipulation of her is yet another form of exploitation; he is another biblical father-figure willing to sacrifice his daughter to save himself and others.

Interestingly enough, God is never mentioned in the book of Esther. Interpreters tend to infer God in the text, arguing that the story shows God at work to ensure Israel's survival. Yet the text itself does not make this claim, opening up space to question whether Esther's sacrifices as a woman are indeed what God wants.

Vashti's and Esther's stories remind us of the coerciveness of sexual abuse. The relational power of Esther's uncle and the political power of the king constrain Esther's choices. We don't know what she wants. Within a very limited context of options, she obeys her uncle and saves her people, but we never know how this may have felt to Esther. Esther's and Vashti's situations are much like those of children and women who are trafficked for sex today, often by family members or boyfriends or mentors. Too often society, including policing and the church, blames the people who are sex trafficked and holds them responsible for their own situations despite the coercive nature of traffickers who prey on vulnerable people. When faith traditions demand obedience to adults, especially adult men, then children and women, especially poor, BIPOC, and queer children and women, become easier targets for trafficking.

Churches also do trafficking victims a disservice when they create rescue narratives to describe outreach to trafficked people. In these cases, the church becomes the proverbial "knight in shining armor" to rescue the "damsel in distress." This image only continues the dehumanization and disempowerment of trafficked people by depicting them as objects in need of rescue rather than agents who lead and participate in their own liberation. Here we can read Esther's story as one in which she works within her constraints to empower herself by speaking to the king. Likewise, rather than thinking of trafficked people as objects in need of rescue, the church should think of them as partners in liberation who should take the lead in their own recovery.

God's People and God's Enemies

Perhaps some of the most troubling passages in the Bible for survivors are those in which we see domestic violence and sexual assault used as metaphors for God's relationship to God's people. These are truly fuzzy, messy, icky passages. What do we make of them?

In the book of Hosea, we find a relationship between Hosea and Gomer that is framed as a picture of God and Israel. The text suggests Hosea is the faithful, long-suffering husband, while Gomer is the unfaithful, adulterous wife. Interestingly enough, this story would have been addressed to Israel, which in the time meant the men of Israel. That means the men of

Israel were supposed to identify with Gomer, making these men the "wife/woman of the divine husband."[49] Certainly, this expectation caused discomfort with its implied threat to traditional heterosexuality and masculinity. Nonetheless, men can also read the text in such a way as to identify with Hosea and express solidarity with his suffering as a victim.[50] We imagine many of us have sat through sermons condemning Gomer and sympathizing with Hosea!

Even more problematic than the way the story presents Gomer as the problem is the way God comes across as a violent abuser. In chapter 2, God threatens to strip Israel naked and expose her, to turn her into a parched land and kill her with thirst. He rages that he will imprison her until she decides to come back to him. Then he will seduce her and speak tenderly to her. This sounds a lot like the cycle of domestic violence, doesn't it? Womanist theologian Renita Weems points out how this passage assumes the validity of marital violence as a way to discipline women. The story shows us a God ready to use violence that, in turn, legitimates men's violence against women and children.[51]

Perhaps the most graphic scene of God's sexual violence against people is in Nahum 3:4–7. In this passage, God calls Nineveh a prostitute or a whore. Throughout the First Testament, this term is leveled at women to discredit them and to frame them as legitimate targets of violence. In particular, raping a prostitute was not a crime because she was not a man's property. Theologian Gerlinde Bauman makes the case from the original language in this passage that the text describes a rape. God, the passage tells us, will rape Nineveh as a way to shame and degrade the city. In fact, the word translated as "devastated" in the NRSV implies complete and utter destruction of the very being of the person described.[52] Finally, we're told that there will be no one to comfort the raped Nineveh. This passage comes within the context of conflict between

Israel and Assyria (Nineveh is Assyria's capital). Not only, then, does the passage justify sexual violence against women, it also justifies rape as a tool of war, a way to subjugate and conquer other people.

The Assyrians have inflicted incredible violence and harm on Israel, and in this book the prophet is turning the situation around so that God now inflicts humiliating sexual violence on the Assyrians, restoring the violated masculinity of the Israelites. Baumann argues that this perspective of victims turned perpetrators is the one Nahum wants readers to assume—he wants us to read it as a "revenge fantasy." Yet survivors know that they still can always be threatened and victimized by sexual violence. They cannot assume that roles can be reversed, and our guess is that most survivors do not want to turn around and perpetuate the same violence against anyone else. And, as Baumann says, certainly this passage is of no comfort to victims of sexual violence in war.[53] Instead, she suggests we read this passage as a text of lament, our lament over the lives of all people devastated by sexual violence.

Again, we should understand this image of God within its historical context. For Nahum's readers (men), this image would have made perfect sense because it falls within the scope of their understandings of gender roles and relations. That does not mean we as modern readers must agree. We can offer critique and reject these images of God as a sexual predator and call on the church to do so as well, especially considering the ways these images are still used so often to justify contemporary violence and sexual abuse.

As we've seen, the First Testament is filled with stories of gender violence, sexual abuse, and rape. Often the text treats women as side notes, characters that simply further the story of men, and objects in transactions between men. These troubling images often become justification for the contemporary church's mistreatment of women, from blaming them for their own abuse to excluding them from leadership in the church. As we've seen in the sex abuse scandals among Catholics, evangelicals, and Southern Baptists, even today religion can enable abuse when people interpret the Bible through white patriarchal lenses.

Fortunately, this is not the only way to interpret the Bible. Feminist Bible scholars offer alternative readings of the text that allow us to name abuse in the very texts that churches most often use to marginalize or exclude women, such as Eve's story. Feminist scholarship also helps us highlight women in the biblical text and try to imagine stories from their perspectives, and feminist biblical criticism points us toward intersectional and decolonizing readings that keep in mind how race, class, and sexuality shape experiences of gender within sexual violence.

CHAPTER 7

Survivors and the Christian Testament

As we turn to the Christian Testament, we find that it, too, tells stories of people victimized through sexual violence. In the gospels we see women who, like the women of the First Testament, have less value than the men around them and are often subject to the whims of more powerful men. Still, we see Jesus including women as disciples and upholding their dignity. By the time of Paul, we discover that the hierarchies of gender, citizenship, and class of the Roman Empire create mixed messages in biblical writings about women and other marginalized people like eunuchs and slaves. The liberating call of the gospel leads to conflicts with dominant ideas about gender and sexuality, and we see this struggle play out in Paul's writings, as well as in the pastoral epistles. Not surprisingly, sexual exploitation and violence are at the center of a number of texts from the Christian Testament.

In the world of the Christian Testament, men exist within the public sphere, while women are confined within the private sphere. Women's concerns are those of home and family, and their and the family's honor is protected by their confinement to the home. Gender is also reinforced by appearance, and, in particular, the dominant culture of the time abhors any deviation from traditional expectations of masculinity and femininity. Effeminate men are especially disparaged in this culture. For a man to act in any way like a woman is considered to be "unnatural."

Mary

You may be surprised to find the mother of Jesus included here as a survivor, but hers is one of those fuzzy, messy, icky stories we have to read honestly and without preconceptions based on what we've always heard. Remember, we can hold multiple and competing interpretations in mind at the same time. So, you don't necessarily have to give up what you've always heard, but letting yourself be uncomfortable with other ideas is a good way to struggle with the complexity of Scripture and sexual violence.

So, why is Mary on this list? Certainly, in Mary's time, people did not have any idea of consent like we do now. At first the property of their fathers and then of their husbands, women really had no rights of their own. They were to be obedient daughters and wives. So we can't simply overlay modern notions of consent over biblical stories. At the same time, however, we do need to make space for those disturbing readings, and Mary's story does ask us to do just that.

Mary's story is usually told as one of an obedient young woman saying yes to God's impregnation of her. Mary is a young teenager at the time of the angel's visit. She's a virgin, betrothed to a man named Joseph, but the angel announces that because God has favored her she will have a son. When she's puzzled how this will be possible, the angel tells her, "The Holy Spirit will come upon you, and the power of the Most High will overshadow you" (Luke 1:35). While Mary assents to God's plan, she's never really asked if it's what she wants, and we must ask if Mary really could have said no even if she wanted to.

First of all, the angel announces the pregnancy as a done deal: "Do not be afraid, Mary, for you have found favor with

God. And now, you will conceive in your womb and bear a son, and you will name him Jesus." It's not a question. Then we have to take into account who sent the message—the Most High God. Brought up as a good Jewish girl, Mary would believe that she is obligated to say yes to God. We also have to consider the imbalance of power between a poor teenage girl in a culture that considered women property and the all-powerful God of Israel.

> *Christa: For most of the time that the pastor was abusing me, which was a period of about seven or eight months, God's power and the pastor's power were intertwined, with the result that, in my mind, the pastor's power grew enormously greater. He was sort of like God's emissary telling me what God wanted, what God's will was. Toward the end of that period, and in the aftermath, God actually changed (meaning that how I thought about God changed). God went dark. God ghosted me. God became untrustworthy. This was not a matter of unbelief, but rather of belief in a God who could be monstrous, immoral and cruel . . . but not always. An unpredictable, uncaring, rejecting, and abusive God who was prone to sadistic whims.*

And just in case anyone thinks Mary doesn't struggle with what is happening to her, remember that she leaves immediately (the Greek says "with haste") to go to her cousin Elizabeth's house. As an unmarried pregnant woman, she is shamed and alone. Elizabeth reminds her of the message, though, that God is with her, and Mary "sings a song of liberation" for all of those who are forced to experience sexual shame.[1] For many survivors, particularly for young, unmarried pregnant women, Mary offers a place for them to identify with sexual shaming and with God's presence on the side of the oppressed.

Debates about the virgin birth aside, the story is really a reflection of cultural attitudes toward women. It is less about God and more about a patriarchal culture that controls and demeans women's sexuality and women's bodies. That no one in that time would have considered the question of consent is telling, and that Mary felt ashamed enough to run off to her cousin's home reminds us of patriarchal judgments about sexuality and bodies.

Now, get ready for this because you may be a bit shocked by this reading. Remember, though, that the point of shocking interpretations is to shake us out of our unexamined assumptions and challenge us to read Scripture in new ways so that we are more empowered to work for transformation in the world. And don't forget, our process is kaleidoscopic—we're holding a lot of tentative and changing ideas in mind all at the same time.

Queer interpretation offers us one important way to think about this story. Argentinian theologian Marcella Althaus-Reid puts it bluntly: the story of Jesus's conception has become the "myth of a woman without a vagina."[2] The story, she says, strips Mary of her sexuality and honors her for subordination to a male God. This reading, then, has been used by the church for centuries to oppress women. She notes especially the ways the Spanish conquerors used an idealized "white lady" image of Mary to subjugate Indigenous people in the Americas.

Instead, Althaus-Reid reads God as queer in this story. She says that God transgresses sexual boundaries by impregnating Mary through "overshadowing" rather than ravishing or penetrating. This, she says, makes God more like queers who break sexual rules and engage in relationships outside the bounds of socially accepted sexuality. Mary reclaims her sexuality by freely choosing to participate in God's transgression of traditional sexual expectations, especially about pregnancy.[3] Within this reading, Mary absolutely has the right to choose, because a queer reading rejects coercion and patriarchal hierarchies. Rather than being subjected to others' decisions about her sexuality, Mary makes her own choice by agreeing to God's transgressive offer of a pregnancy outside of marriage.

Survivors read this story in these multiple ways. If we read Mary as without power to consent, we may identify with our own sense of powerlessness before the God of patriarchy. This is particularly true for survivors of sexual abuse by godlike figures such as pastors and fathers. These survivors often could not say no, or their "no" was ignored. Still, we can find in Mary's song of liberation hope for freedom, as we can in queer and feminist interpretations that focus on Mary's agency. Again, no one simple reading will do. Survivors help us see the many possibilities for understanding Mary and for finding in Mary a place to see ourselves and feel seen, to wrestle with God's role in our abuse, and to create hope in God's presence and liberating work in the world.

Grace: Biblical stories hold truth. But not necessarily the truth known as "absolute truth" or "divine truth" that we may have been taught at church. I was taught by my parents and the Korean Presbyterian Church to read the Bible literally. There were no other ways to approach the Bible if you were to be a "true" Christian. Therefore, it took a long time for me to unpack some of the underlying truths behind the biblical stories and read the Bible with different interpretive tools.

The story of Mary is a difficult one for me. I was always taught to "be like Mary" and be submissive to God. Submission to God is a patriarchal reading and approach to this story. An intersectional reading of the Bible (which we share in our book, Intersectional Theology) provides a deeper insight and kaleidoscopic approach to the story of Mary. Using different approaches to reading the Bible and taking into account cultural contexts and biases has become an empowering way for me to read Scripture. These different interpretive tools have become liberating for me in reading the story of Mary. If we implement these tools, these biblical stories can be freeing and hopeful to us during our darkest times of anguish and agony.

The Woman Who Was Almost Stoned

Jesus is teaching in the Temple when a group of religious leaders confronts him to test him. They bring an unidentified woman to him whom they say they have caught in the act of adultery. Biblical scholar Jennifer Garcia Bashaw points out that we trust these religious leaders are telling the truth, but they bring no witnesses nor the woman's partner. She notes, "Even if she is as guilty as they say, we should at least be wary of the religious leaders' motives. Yet most of us aren't. We assume the woman is guilty because our ecclesial history has consistently reminded us of women's guilt."[4] According to the Law of Moses, the religious leaders explain, she should be stoned to death. They ask Jesus what he thinks. Stoning under Mosaic Law was an orderly and rational procedure and was conducted as a court-ordered form of capital punishment.

That's not what we see in this story. We see a potential lynching. In Christian Testament times, the Roman government reserved the power to approve all capital punishments, and even if the Romans granted the Jews permission to conduct an execution, they may not have allowed stoning to be the method.[5] In the case of this woman brought before Jesus, clearly, her accusers are not coming from nor going to a formal trial. They are a mob who have decided to take matters into their own hands. They want a lynching.[6]

Interestingly enough, the mob has not brought the man with her, even though Mosaic Law commanded both be put to death. This passage, like so many others, reinforces male judgment and control of women's sexuality. This woman has acted with sexual agency, and that is a threat to the system of patriarchy and so must be snuffed out in the harshest way possible to send a clear message.

In this instance, however, the mob is really interested in implicating Jesus in some way. They want to see if he'll follow Mosaic Law and participate in the violence or if he'll challenge

Mosaic Law and set himself up for theological trouble. Jesus does neither. He writes in the sand, effectively taking the spotlight off the woman. Then he tells the crowd that the one of them without sin should cast the first stone. One by one, they walk away until only Jesus and the woman are left.

Many feminists read this as a story of Jesus siding with women against the structures of patriarchy. While there's a danger in turning the story into a tale of a knight in shining armor rescuing a damsel in distress, we can instead read this story as one of Jesus's challenge to patriarchy. Adultery is considered an offense against the husband to whom the woman belongs. His honor and the honor of the male community have been impugned by her assertion of her own sexuality, which challenges men's rights to control women's sexuality. Jesus, however, refuses to participate in the patriarchal demand for this woman's death. In so doing, he also refuses to join them in reestablishing male honor by stoning her. In fact, Jesus is willing to lose male honor to restore this woman's honor, just as he is willing to become a victim of the patriarchal order in order to overturn it. Jesus puts adultery on the same level as the sins committed by the men who condemn this woman. In fact, he treats the men in the group just as he does the woman, thereby offering a reordering of the social system in which both women and men have the same opportunities to confront their sins and choose a new way of living. In essence, as one scholar puts it, the story suggests that men should quit proclaiming their sinlessness in relation to women and should admit their own sinful involvement with patriarchy. They should follow Jesus and break with patriarchy. This story, then, becomes an invitation to men to join in Jesus's radical social reordering.[7]

This reading of the story sends a strong message to contemporary Christian men about their responsibility for ending sexism and sexual violence. Men need to recognize all the ways they participate in and benefit from a culture of sexual violence and renounce the sexism and misogyny that maintain sexual violence. Men need to address the violence of other men. This story speaks particularly to men in purity culture who hold women and girls responsible for men's sexuality, including their sexual abuse of women. As this story suggests, these men should stop proclaiming their sexual sinlessness and confess their own sinful involvement with sexism and sexual violence.

Enslaved Boys

"What enslaved boys?" you may be asking. That's because too often translators and interpreters have misused I Corinthians 6:9–10 to malign queer people. In this passage, Paul uses two ancient Greek words that are very problematic for translators, *malakoi* and *arsenokoitai*. No one is completely sure what they mean. The King James Version translates *malakoi* as "effeminate" and *arsenokoitai* as "abusers of themselves with mankind." The Revised Standard Version of 1946 and 1952 arbitrarily combines these words and renders them "homosexuals." The original language, however, makes no reference to sexual orientations. In fact, Paul's world has no concept of sexual orientations. Moral concerns were about actions, not orientations. The words actually seem to single out specific kinds of sexual practices that Paul considers deplorable. The New International Version combines the words and renders them "men who have sex with men," explaining that this term captures what the words mean—the active (penetrative) and passive (receptive) participants. Some translators, however, argue that the words do not refer to egalitarian and consensual sex. In fact, our conception of male same-sex relationships would have been unthinkable for Roman citizens (only certain men were citizens). Culture dictated that Roman citizens only have sex with their inferiors—women, slaves, prostitutes, boys, and girls. And for them, it matters who's on top. The penetrative role is the masculine role. To be penetrated is to be inferior. To imagine an egalitarian relationship when one partner is penetrative and the other receptive is impossible. Instead of translating these words to refer to homosexuality, many translators argue that the words refer to male prostitutes and the men who use them.

During this time, wealthy men often kept both wives and enslaved boys they used to gratify their sexual desires. In fact, some of these boys may have been kidnapped specifically for the purpose of sexual servitude. Some interpreters argue that Paul is criticizing the exploitation he sees in this accepted system of sex trafficking. They identify these verses as addressing the men who use boys for sex and the enslavers who procure these boys.

This final translation, which we find most compelling, can speak today directly to the Catholic Church's priest abuse scandal as well as the global trafficking of children for sex. In 2002, an investigative journalist team for the *Boston Globe* uncovered not only the widespread abuse of children, especially boys, by Catholic priests but also the enablers in church hierarchy who ignored complaints, concealed accusations, and moved abusers around to protect them and the church. Still today, new accounts of abuse and cover-up are coming to light, even as the church continues to fail to address the overwhelming needs of survivors and make the deep structural changes needed to prevent abuse. The fallout has had tremendous impact on victims. One victim, Mike, says, "They stole the most sacred thing I had, and that was my Catholic Church." Another victim, Carolyn adds, "The word 'God' makes me think of him. I just feel like my whole life has been a lie. . . . It's very lonely, especially when it's your word against God's."[8]

Unhappy Endings: Not All Victims Survive

Many of us who have experienced sexual violence choose to refer to ourselves as survivors because we recognize the strength we used to get through what happened to us. Some of us, however, use the term "victim" because "survivor" doesn't always capture the initial violence and ongoing trauma of sexual abuse. The term "survivor" can also make people who have been victimized feel judged or inadequate if they have not overcome their abuse. Survivor narratives often make healing seem an incredible feat of strength and resilience that is the only right path for people who have experienced sexual abuse, and people who do not feel they are healing or who cannot overcome their trauma may feel like failures because they do not have a narrative of success. In fact, they may feel like they're being told they just need to "get over it" and move on rather than experience the very real effects of PTSD, physical injury, and thoughts of suicide. The goal is not one of overcoming sexual abuse but of learning to live with it as a central feature of our experience that shapes us in many ways. We have to figure out how to embrace that part of our histories and integrate it rather than reject it. That takes time and may never happen fully. In some ways, we are always victims, even when we are survivors.

Seeing the perspectives of victims, rather than survivors, may disrupt feminist tendencies to read stories of biblical victims as simple narratives of patriarchal violence, women's overcoming, and eventually God's justice. We know the long-reaching effects of sexual abuse don't always follow this pattern. Sometimes the accusers don't drop their stones and walk away; not all victims become a queen who saves her people or a girl who gives birth to a savior. Sometimes victims don't recover; there's no justice; God's nowhere to be seen; and, as difficult as this reality is, we have to consider it because many people live with it, and their experiences have something different to tell us about God.

Another central reality is that not all victims survive. Some die, violently, despicably, finally. These are more than Phyllis Trible's "sad stories."[9] These are people whose lives are cut short by sexual violence, and, in our thinking about God, we have to take account of stories with unhappy, unsatisfying, unhelpful endings.[10]

The Christian Testament has unhappy stories for women. Revelation imagines the Roman Empire as Babylon, a "whore" who has seduced the kings of the earth into committing fornication with her and who has corrupted the earth. God's response is to "give her the wine-cup of the fury of his wrath" (Revelation 16:19). An angel announces, "Fallen, fallen is Babylon the great! It has become a dwelling-place of demons, a haunt of every foul spirit, a haunt of every foul bird, a haunt of every foul and hateful beast" (Revelation 18:2), and threatens, "her plagues will come in a single day—pestilence and mourning and famine—and she will be burned with fire" (Revelation 18:8).

To find perhaps the unhappiest story of all, we return to the First Testament and a story in Judges 19. In this story, a Levite has taken a woman. Even the use of the verb "take" here suggests the story starts in sexual violence against a woman. The story calls her a concubine, but many scholars argue that she was a secondary wife.[11] At some point, she leaves the Levite and goes back to her father's house. Some translations say she prostituted herself, but other translations say she was angry with her husband.[12] In that time, because women were their husbands' property, for a woman to take the initiative to leave would have been perceived as an act of unfaithfulness. As the story goes on, we see she likely did not have an affair because the Levite goes to her father's house to try to win her back. Now, already by asserting her sexual agency and leaving the Levite, in that time, she had shamed him and insulted his masculinity. Now, at her father's house, her father, who may have been protecting her, keeps delaying their departure, which some interpreters read as a way her father was either protecting her or asserting his own power over the Levite, further shaming him.[13]

At last they leave late in the day, and so they need to stop overnight. The Levite refuses to stop in the town of foreigners and goes on to Gibeah, a town of Benjaminites. According to the norms of hospitality, people should offer strangers refuge, but not until late into the night does someone do so. The Levite and his wife go to the home of the man, and soon there's a knock at the door, and the men of the city are there demanding the homeowner turn over the Levite so they can rape him.

This is not an act of homosexual sexuality. It is an act of violence. It's about enhancing one's honor at the expense of the honor of other men.[14] For people of that time, men raping men is a way to assert masculinity and dominance. To treat another man like a woman is to shame him and to lessen his masculinity. Hospitality norms mean the homeowner should protect his guest, and so he refuses to turn the man over. Instead he offers the angry mob his virgin daughter and the Levite's wife. At this point, the man chooses hospitality norms over the humanity of the women in his house. Yet, the angry mob refuses the offer because the story is not about the women but about men exerting power over one another. The story then takes an even uglier turn. The Levite throws his wife out the door to the mob who gang rape her all night. Some interpreters suggest this part of the story also reinforces women's status as property. The virgin daughter of the man, who is perceived as innocent and living within the confines of patriarchal control, is spared by the story. The Levite's wife, who asserted her agency by leaving him, is punished for daring to resist constraint.

After her rape, the woman manages to crawl to the doorstep, where the Levite finds her the next morning. At this point the story is unclear if she is already dead or not, but the Levite loads her onto a donkey and takes her home.[15] When he gets home he plunges a knife into her and cuts her into twelve pieces, which he sends to the tribes of Israel to provoke a war against the tribe of Benjamin.

Susan: Whenever I do this kind of close biblical reading and turn to biblical scholars for insight, I'm always surprised at how I still bring so many assumptions to the text. As I read scholars about this passage who pointed out that the text doesn't make clear when the woman died, I had one of those moments of surprise. Even as a child, I had read this story that the Levite kills the woman when he gets home. That image from childhood kept me from even seeing that the text doesn't say if she dies then or as a result of the injuries sustained in her assault. Now I find myself thinking about the story and hoping she was dead before they left Gibeah so she didn't have to suffer one more indignity at the hands of her husband. Of course, either way, she is still dead. There's no surviving this story. She's just dead.

What do we do with this? Among many of us is the inclination to rush to resurrection, heaven, eternal bliss in the stead of abuse, violence, and death. But what if we sit with this story for a while? What if we let ourselves be unhappy with it? Unhappy with what happened, unhappy with the ending, unhappy with the absence of God for this woman, unhappy with death. What might we learn from not rushing to the sweet by-and-by as a way to avoid the cold, hard reality of gendered violent death? What does God look like when there's no happy ending?

We can't impose a happy ending on this story either. The text doesn't allow it. Certainly, the text is critical of the situation. The story is framed with a condemnation of every man doing "what was right in his own eyes," and the narrator calls the men of Gibeah "a perverse lot." The blame is squarely on the men in the story. Nothing in the text suggests the woman is to blame.

Yet, despite her blamelessness, we can't assume God comforted her, that she felt God near. We can't negate the awfulness of this story by putting her in a heaven of our own making. She'd have had no concept of such a thing as we imagine it. We just need to sit with the horror of this story for a while and let it be horrific. That's really hard for Christians to do sometimes. Often, we think we're not being faithful if we are depressed or grieving or angry, and for victims of sexual abuse this can add trauma to their trauma by making them feel guilty that they can't simply pray the trauma away.

What do we do with this unhappy story and its unhappy ending with all it may suggest about God and the world?

> *Susan: For me, the ending of this story reflects the truth that sometimes evil wins. I don't mean a devil or some external entity. I mean the evil that human beings do when they dehumanize, use, and abuse others. Grace is the one who taught me the word for the feelings I have about this—han—the suffering that comes with unresolved injustice. Sometimes we are not going to be healed; sometimes goodness and justice will not triumph. There's no meaning in the Levite's wife's death—she doesn't even get her own name—no lesson to be learned, no redemption, no salvation. There's only death. And even in her death her body gets used to start a war that will bring about more rape, more suffering, and more death.*
>
> *I think sitting with this despair honors her (and our) suffering, anguish, grief, and death by not minimizing just how horrific it is, by not turning it into some narrative of triumph, because not all victims triumph, not all victims survive.*

In our own time we have an epidemic of missing and murdered Indigenous women and girls in the United States and Canada. Every year, thousands of Indigenous women and girls go missing or are murdered. In fact, murder is the third leading cause of death for Indigenous women and girls aged ten to twenty-four.[16] The murder rate for women in some tribal communities is ten times the national average. More than half of all Indigenous women experience sexual assault at some point in their lifetimes, and 80 percent have experienced some kind of gender-based violence. Most are harmed by non-Indigenous men. This crisis is rooted in the United States' history of colonization and genocide and its ongoing anti-Indigenous racism. Zones of contact between Indigenous people and colonizers have always been fraught and dangerous, especially for women. Today, most Indigenous people do not live on tribal lands but in cities where they are constantly in contact with the dominant culture, making them especially vulnerable to sexual violence within this contact zone. Yet, while the numbers are shocking—over five thousand Indigenous women and girls go missing each year—the dominant culture has taken little notice. Few people outside of Indigenous communities care. This is an unhappy story with multiple unhappy endings as bodies are discovered—or not—year after year after year.

Grace: In times of despair, we lament. We cry out to God in our pain, suffering, agony, and brokenness. There is nothing more that we can do, and our pain is too deep. It breaks our bodies, our souls, and our being. In our torment, we turn to God and lament. Lament is not practiced much within our churches or in our personal lives. But it is biblical and something that the Israelites had practiced.

Lament is a passionate expression of grief, and when one carries han, *it can be expressed through wailing, moaning, and weeping. It is a cry from within the depths of our suffering. Lament is a small step toward some sort of healing. During World War II when Japanese soldiers kidnapped and took young Korean girls to be comfort women (sexual slaves), many died due to the gravity of the sexual assaults which occurred forty to seventy times a day. There is a story of young girls who realized that they were being kidnapped to become sexual slaves to the Japanese soldiers. They made their escape and lamented their lives and jumped off a huge cliff to their deaths.*

Lament needs to be part of our narrative to share and explore the gravity of acts committed against our bodies. Sexual assault not only affects our bodies; it affects our minds and our souls. Due to the enormous burden on our souls, we lament and cry out to God for healing, peace, and recovery.

Biblical survivors present us with some really difficult questions about who God is. Certainly, the biblical record reflects the violence of patriarchy characteristic of biblical times—and ours. Although we may see that God is with biblical survivors, we don't often get much of a sense of justice for survivors, or for those who did not survive. In fact, we may be left with a greater sense of *han* than anything else after we read their stories.

These stories mostly aren't particularly inspiring for victims and survivors. They don't often make God look that great in relation to women either. So, what's their usefulness for us? The presence of these victims and survivors in the Bible can help us feel seen. We see that others have also suffered, that they have not always survived and thrived, that they have not had answers to their suffering or divine intervention to save them from abuse and trauma. We're not alone. We can sit with these stories and let them speak to us by opening ourselves up to see them with new eyes that don't assume we already know what's in the story. We can read with tentativeness, knowing the point isn't getting to the "one right interpretation" but listening for the text to speak to us where we are.

Sitting with unhappiness offers us a kind of freedom. We don't have to deny or negate our sadness, depression, grief, or rage. We don't have to pretend everything is all right. We don't have to act happy and say, "God's in heaven; all's right with the world." We're free from the expectations of a sunny kind of Christianity that ignores the impact of traumatic events so we're free to feel what we feel and think what we think and be okay with that. In these unhappy biblical stories, we can find a kind of community of sufferers and of victims.

Novelist Walker Percy explained that if an alienated commuter on a train is reading about an alienated commuter on a train, the reader overcomes alienation by finding community with the character in the book.[17] Likewise, when we read in the Bible stories about people like ourselves, we find community, even when the story is unhappy. We can feel seen and understood because we see characters who are like us, and, in so doing, we can begin to embrace our own experiences and understand God as one who also suffers with us. After all, many of God's stories are unhappy ones too.

CHAPTER 8

Jesus the Survivor

Susan: In all my years in church, in seminary, in teaching religion, no one ever suggested to me that Jesus had experienced sexual abuse and sexual assault. The first I heard of this was when I started researching this book and read the historical scholarship on crucifixion. Realizing that Roman soldiers in all likelihood sexually assaulted Jesus was like a gut punch. My sorrow for the beaten, battered, crucified, and sexually assaulted Jesus nearly overwhelmed me. He had suffered the humiliation and trauma of sexual abuse amid his torture, and I felt a new kind of grief for him . . . and another layer of anger at what the church had covered up. I felt again like my students in Feminism in the Bible who often ask, "Why has no one ever told me this before?"

Grace: Sexual abuse was never talked about in the church or home. It was a taboo subject in Korean American churches and within immigrant homes. Abuse and sexuality are topics which are pushed aside as unimportant. It was believed that if you don't talk about it, it will "just go away." People just felt it was unnecessary to share their own stories of sexual abuse or assault as it would bring shame to them and their families. Due to shame associated with sexual assault, it was never discussed in the church. Everyone was ashamed to talk about such a terrible subject in the church.

Topics surrounding human sexuality, sexual violence, and rape are taboo topics, and as a result, they will never be talked about or associated with Jesus. The mere possibility of sexual violence committed against Jesus was unimaginable. It would be sacrilegious to even consider this as a possibility of what happened to Jesus during the physical abuse before he was nailed to the cross.

Why hadn't either one of us ever heard that the Romans more than likely would have sexually assaulted Jesus? Why hadn't Sunday school teachers, seminary professors, or pastors talked about this? We imagine a number of reasons behind this, reasons that continue to affect today's survivors—from Christian shame around sexuality to fear of violated masculinity to disbelief that Jesus would have experienced such a thing. Within patriarchy, sexual violation makes men feel emasculated. Patriarchy cannot allow such a thing to happen to God's son, who is viewed as lord, savior, and triumphant Christ who will come again. The very idea of a sexually violated Jesus goes against the central ideas the church has created of a white male savior who comes into the world to save us from our sinful ways for a better world to come. Yet, the historical evidence is clear—more likely than not, Jesus was sexually assaulted by Roman soldiers.

Crucifixion and Sexual Shaming in the Roman Empire

Rome was an imperial power that conquered and colonized a great deal of what is now Europe. In order to maintain control over conquered people, the Roman Empire utilized a number of violent mechanisms of state terror, including sexual humiliation, sexual assault, and crucifixion. Crucifixions weren't simply individual punishments; rather, they functioned as a reminder of Rome's power over entire peoples as a way to prevent challenges and rebellion against the empire. So, Romans mostly used crucifixions, not against Roman citizens, but against slaves and other subjugated people who might contest Roman authority.[1] Crucifixions were clear reminders of what could happen to people if they defied the empire.

Crucifixion was a public ordeal that could last for days. It was a cruel form of capital punishment that led to a slow death from asphyxiation. In addition to its physical tortures, it created incredible shaming. Victims were naked as they were crucified. Sometimes, their genitals were impaled, or they were castrated. As theologian David Tombs points out, for men, crucifixion was a metaphorical emasculation. He writes, "In a patriarchal society, where men competed against each other to display virility in terms of sexual power over others, the public display of the naked victim by the 'victors' in front of onlookers and passers-by carried the message of sexual domination."[2] The shame of being nailed naked to a wooden beam in front of a crowd must have been unbearable. Criminals were crucified in public places on a hill so that everyone could see them publicly and witness their painful deaths.

Before crucifixion, victims were tortured. They were mocked, beaten, stripped naked, flogged, sexually humiliated, and likely sexually assaulted. The evidence for sexual assault comes from what we know about military life in the Roman Empire and elsewhere, rather than from direct description by writers at the time. Across history, we've seen that colonizers use sexual assault as a way to subjugate and control conquered people. We also know that in the ancient world anal rape of captured men was a common practice of dominance. Roman soldiers lived a highly regimented and hierarchical military life where they were at the bottom of the military order. Their superiors had absolute power over them, and, as we know from history, when men are subjected to feelings of powerlessness they often enact brutal power over less powerful others. Often, in military life across the centuries, this exertion of power over others has manifested in sexual violence.

For example, in Guatemala's thirty-six-year internal armed conflict, which we mentioned in chapter 1, the military and paramilitary organizations systematically used rape to subjugate Indigenous Mayans. One of the places where this happened was a military outpost in Sepur Zarco, where Indigenous Maya

Q'eqchi men and boys were often "disappeared" and women were enslaved and raped. In 2011, fifteen survivors of Sepur Zarco took their case to court, setting a world precedent for a court ruling on sexual enslavement during armed conflict. In finding in favor of the women, the court noted that rape and sexual assault were deliberate strategies by the Guatemalan army to disrupt and discourage Indigenous communities who were struggling for land, water, and resource rights. We have also seen rape used as a tool of war in Rwanda, where sexual violence, torture, mutilation, and enslavement were used against Tutsi women as weapons of genocide. In Darfur, Sudanese forces used rape as a form of ethnic cleansing against African tribes to destroy families and communities. In Bosnia, Serbs used places like police stations and sports centers to carry out mass rapes. The hotel Vilina Vlas, just outside of Višegrad, held possibly two hundred Bosniak girls and women who were systematically raped to become pregnant by Serbs. Men are also victims of rape in contemporary wars, although they are much more likely to stay silent about it. In the Congo, men were captured and raped multiple times each day. Other instances of the rape of men as a tool of war come from Sri Lanka, Chile, Croatia, Iran, Kuwait, and the former Yugoslavia. The examples show the critical link between militaries and sexual assault, underlining the likelihood that Roman soldiers, too, participated in sexual violence as a way to humiliate, dominate, dehumanize, and subjugate colonized people.

The Sexually Assaulted Jesus

David: Their "suffering" theology kept me bound in self-hate, self-harm, guilt, and shame. What I have since learned has taught me to love myself and others for who we are. SBC fundamentalist theology taught me to despise myself. I have since come to understand Jesus anew. And to understand the suffering I endured was not because of anything wrong I had done, but because crimes were committed against me.

At the very least, we know that Jesus was stripped naked and suffered sexual shaming. Given what we know about Roman crucifixion, we can imagine with some certainty, even though the biblical texts don't tell us for sure, that Jesus was sexually assaulted and probably raped. We can guess that Jesus's sexual assault was too much for the gospel writers to contemplate: too horrific, too emasculating, too embarrassing for the church.

Yet from survivors' perspectives, we know that Jesus's sexual assault is important in the way that it further identifies Jesus with those of us without patriarchal power—women, BIPOC, queers. In his poem "Jesus in Abu Ghraib," Pádraig Ó Tuama writes:

The way to be a man is
not to be a girl, so the
way to break a man is to
make him a girl, or
some other kind of animal.
Dress him up, or down, or
turn him round and bend him
over. Make him show her
what he doesn't want to show
her. Make him beg
for what she will not give.
Bag his head, but not his body
Yet. Wait. Shame him. And again.
Take a picture. Smile.[3]

Similarly, many queer theologians identify Jesus with Matthew Shephard, the young gay man murdered in 1998. He was left hanging on a fence by the road to die just outside

Laramie, Wyoming. In sexually shamed, violated, broken, and murdered bodies we can see Jesus, and we understand that his death was about patriarchal power and the need for a violent colonizer to destroy any threat to that power.

Jesus's suffering, however, is not a model for us. As African theologians have pointed out, holding up Jesus's suffering as a model simply serves the causes of colonization. *Mujerista* theologian Ada Maria Isasi-Díaz says that a central value of liberation for Latinas is *la lucha*, the struggle. She is quick to point out, however, that embracing the struggle is not the same as accepting suffering. In fact, she says that the notion of suffering as necessary, redemptive, or God's will is a control mechanism that dominant groups use to help maintain power and control over oppressed peoples. She says Latinas don't go about their everyday lives thinking about suffering but rather about how to survive. Instead of thinking of themselves as suffering, Latinas think of themselves as engaged in struggle. Evidence of this is in Latinas' capacity for celebration, *la fiesta*. These are not celebrations *of* suffering but celebrations *against* suffering.[4] Similarly, we can think about Pride parades which are both protest and celebration.

To accept suffering, or worse yet, in some Christian traditions, to positively glorify it, is to assume a kind of masochism that is self-defeating and self-destructive. We cannot extol suffering, neither ours nor Jesus's, as a solution to sexual violence.

> *Shanell: If Jesus was God's son, then why . . . ? Was humanity—with all our sinfulness—worth the sexualized trauma he experienced? Did he still trust God when he hung on the cross bleeding and naked as the day he was born . . .*
>
> *If God is all-knowing, all-powerful, and all-seeing, then why did God not do something? Why did God allow my assailant to do those things to me? Why did God not deliver me from this man?*

This supposed God-fearing man? This church leader who to this day preaches and reads Scripture from the pulpit. I am a daughter of the church! I am God's child. And yet . . . I laid there. Like Jesus hung there. There was no deliverance for me either. Not then. Not now . . .

I do not take comfort in knowing that Jesus died with sexual trauma as a main component of his torture. Am I supposed to find solidarity with Jesus because he experienced sexual trauma like me? Where is the "good news" in that? . . .

I wish neither one of us experienced that![5]

God does not want us to suffer. God did not want Jesus to experience sexual shaming and assault, and God does not want us to experience these things either. God wants us to flourish and to thrive. God wants to repair the damage we've experienced because of sexual violence. We cannot say that since Jesus suffered it is all right for us to suffer. Rather, we must say that because we see the injustice in Jesus's suffering, we also see it in our own.

Jesus Forsaken

Suffering is not redemptive. Granted, that's probably not what most of us have heard at church. We've heard how God required Jesus's suffering, how Jesus suffered in our place, how Jesus paid for our sins because God demanded a blood sacrifice to atone for humanity's sinfulness. We've sung "Jesus paid it all," "To God be the glory, great things he has done! So loved he the world that he gave us his Son, who yielded his life an atonement for sin," and "O Jesus, Lord and Savior, I give myself to Thee, For Thou, in Thine atonement, didst give Thyself for me."

The notion of atonement is found within both the First and Christian Testaments, and these are the texts many theologians and pastors, especially those in dominant social groups, center in their understandings of Jesus's suffering. Ancient Jews understood atonement was a way for people to purify themselves from sinfulness, starting with their own hearts and being demonstrated through sacrifice. It was about reconciling oneself to God.

There are three main types of atonement in the Hebrew Scriptures: Paschal Lamb, sacrificial system, and the Day of Atonement. These understandings of atonement offer only temporary forgiveness, and *korbanot* (offerings, part of the sacrificial system) could only be used as a means of atoning for the lightest type of sin, that is, sins committed in ignorance. There were three kinds of *korbanot*—animals, grain, and money (Leviticus 5:11, 5:18, and 14:21)—which were offered up to God.[6] The word *korban* means "something which draws close." And the purpose of atonement was to bring people closer to God. After the destruction of the Temple in 70 CE, Jewish people stopped offering *korbanot*. The rabbis began to teach that prayer brought them closer to God rather than sacrifices.[7]

A much more troubling notion of sacrifice is prominently displayed in the terrifying story of God telling Abraham to offer up his son, Isaac. We read this story and wonder how God could possibly request such a sacrifice. "God tested Abraham. He said to him, 'Abraham!' And he said, 'Here I am.' He said, 'Take your son, your only son Isaac, whom you love, and go to the land of Moriah and offer him there as a burnt offering on one of the mountains that I shall show you'" (Genesis 22:1–2). God's command to Abraham to sacrifice Isaac makes our stomachs turn, as it is violent, aggressive, and disturbing. We question whether God is a loving God or a dangerous God that demands sacrifices of our sons.

A Jewish poet reads the story this way:

> *The real hero of the Isaac story was the ram,*
> *who didn't know about the conspiracy between the others.*
> *As if he had volunteered to die instead of Isaac.*

I want to sing a song in his memory—
about his curly wool and his human eyes,
about the horns that were silent on his living head,
and how they made those horns into shofars when he was
    slaughtered
to sound their battle cries
or to blare out their obscene joy. . . .
The angel went home.
Isaac went home.
Abraham and God had gone long before.

But the real hero of the Isaac story
was the ram.[8]

In this telling, the poet reminds us that someone else may well have to bear the burden of others' choices, that what seems heroic or godly may only mask the harm to someone else. We have to wonder if God actually ever wanted any kind of sacrifice.

Early Christian interpreters took the idea of atonement and then reshaped it to try to understand what happened to Jesus. In one way or another, many of these theories of atonement focused on the idea that God needed something from Jesus in order to redeem humankind. For example, the satisfaction theory, which was articulated by Anselm of Canterbury in the twelfth century and is the official position of the Catholic Church, says that humanity's sin has offended God, and so recompense must be made to satisfy God's justice. An earlier theory, the ransom theory, held that, essentially, Adam and Eve had sold humanity out to the devil through their sin in the garden, and so a ransom had to be paid to the devil to buy humanity back. Later ransom theorists argued that humanity had to be bought back from the bondage of sin, not the devil per se.

Perhaps the theory that holds greatest currency in contemporary evangelical life is the penal substitutionary atonement theory. This theory argues that God's righteousness required punishment for sin for every human being, that God needed a blood sacrifice to appease God's wrath. Jesus became the substitute for humanity and took on all of God's wrath and punishment on our behalf; he bore the punishment we should have had for our sin.

From the perspectives of survivors, these ideas of atonement are highly problematic because they suggest that brutality, violence, and murder can be required by God; they justify the use of brute power and violence to meet some expectation or requirement of retribution and punishment. They picture God as willing the torture, rape, and death of Jesus to satisfy God. Was Jesus really sexually assaulted for us? Does God's need for violent punishment mean God would will our torture, rape, and death had Jesus not died on the cross? Some Christians might say yes. That's exactly what hell is: a place of eternal torture. We wonder if these people also imagine hell as a place of eternal sexual abuse. Again, we return to our earlier question about what kind of God would demand this. Do we really imagine that a God of love, a parent, even a wrathful one, would send children for eternity to such a place? Even if we imagine Jesus as our substitute, his suffering lasted only a few days. How does that compare with an eternity of suffering? Are these actually equal in God's sight? Parents may punish children, yet we cannot imagine any parent who would consign a child, no matter how rebellious, to the tortures of hell for eternity. What parent would even conceive of such a place? So why do we want to think that God would, especially when the Bible itself offers us alternative ways to understand God and the death of Jesus?

If we look closely at all the stories and descriptions of God in the Bible, we get different images. God is a mother hen who takes her chicks under her wings. "How often have I desired to gather your children together as a hen gathers her brood under her wings" (Matthew 23:37). God is a spirit hovering over the water, an artist constructing a human from mud, wisdom, a mother birthing her children (Deuteronomy 32:18), nursing her young (Isaiah 49:15), protecting them (Deuteronomy 32:11–12), comforting them (Isaiah 66:13), feeding them and lifting them to her cheek (Hosea 11:3–4). From such images, we can imagine different understandings of Jesus's death on the cross, that his death was not God's need for satisfaction, not a substitution for us, the rightful victims of God's violence.

So how do we understand what happened to Jesus?

Images of God as violent are rooted in patriarchal notions of power and dominance. Within patriarchy, violence is a primary mechanism for gaining and maintaining power. God exerts power over humanity by demanding punishment, and God shows God's ultimate power by demanding death. It may help survivors of sexual abuse if we recognize that traditional images emphasizing a God of wrath and punishment reflect patriarchal power and serve to maintain patriarchal power in the hands of powerful men, especially powerful men who can abuse, torture, rape, and kill. Rather than a reality, a true depiction of the nature of God, these images of wrath, punishment, and violence reflect what powerful and dominant men have, want, and use to hold onto their place in society, especially in relation to "lesser" people—women, LGBTQ people, BIPOC, people with disabilities, poor people. This is a God who can enable, justify, overlook, and excuse sexual abuse, rape, and murder by real men because God required these things to happen to Jesus to attain salvation for all.

If, however, we see God as love, cosufferer, space to grieve, a child, relational, a way out of no way, mothering, queer, and accompaniment, we cannot accept images of God as a punishing and violent power, who, through God's demands for satisfaction or retribution, abuses Jesus.

If we return to the gospels and their historical context, we see that Jesus was a threat to dominant religious and political powers of his day. Jesus challenged distortions of faith that valued keeping laws over loving people, that ignored marginalized people, and that kept abusive power in place through oppressive systems.

Jesus was becoming a threat. He was teaching about God's kingdom, a present and in-breaking community of love and justice. He hung out with society's outcasts; he preached against exploitation, worldly might, and oppression. At the time, many Jews were part of a political movement against the Romans. These zealots engaged in protests, strikes, and riots in resistance to the Roman Empire. The gospels tell us that one of Jesus's disciples was Simon the Zealot. Obviously, Jesus's message resonated as a political message of freedom from colonization. Romans in Jerusalem would have had little patience with anything they perceived as rabble-rousing among the zealots. Some biblical scholars think Judas may have been a zealot. He betrayed Jesus, thinking Jesus would resist and begin the revolution against the Romans. This would explain why Judas committed suicide after Jesus was condemned. His plan had backfired. Rather than forcing Jesus's hand to start the revolution, Judas's betrayal had only led to Jesus's death.

From this perspective, we see that Jesus died, not because God needed to punish someone, but because Jesus spoke out on the side of the poor and oppressed, the marginalized and disenfranchised. The Romans saw Jesus as a potential threat to their political power. That's why they crucified him. His death wasn't needed to change how God looks at us; his death was inevitable because he challenged religious and political power with his message of love and justice. The resurrection was God's affirmation of Jesus and his message.

Grace: I was always taught in church that Jesus died because of our sins. God needed to punish us, but instead Jesus took our place. Across my education, I learned about various theories of atonement, most of which are all variations of this type of understanding of the crucifixion. It was only much later, after I started teaching theology myself, that I learned that this may not be why Jesus died on the cross.

Understanding God as a fearful and punishing God perpetuates a patriarchal God and a power-hungry God who dominates over us. There are plenty of biblical references which teach us otherwise. They tell us that God loves us beyond human understanding, and nothing can separate us from the love of God. "For I am convinced that neither death, nor life, nor angels, nor rulers, nor things present, nor things to come, nor powers, nor height, nor depth, nor anything else in all creation will be able to separate us from the love of God in Christ Jesus our Lord" (Romans 8:38–39). If we focus on God's love for us, we can move away from images of a fearful, punishing, and cruel God. Instead, we see a loving and just God who suffered with Jesus and then affirmed him through his resurrection.

Doubting Jesus

No one doubts that Jesus was wronged. Monica Poole points out that we don't go over Jesus's behavior to figure out what he did wrong; we don't justify the acts of the Roman Empire; we don't argue that Jesus shouldn't have created such a spectacle by parading into the city or disrupting the marketplace at the Temple or calling out religious leaders. We don't blame Jesus for not speaking up on his own behalf.[9] Why, then, Poole wonders, do we respond this way to contemporary victims?

Dawn: Between the ages of seven and eight I was being molested by an uncle. Simultaneously, in the evenings, my sister and I would say nightly prayers with my great-grandmother and great-aunt. While I always remember my great-aunt to speak kindly about God, my great-grandmother was unpredictable and often warned us not to disobey and anger "Him." I knew that she was aware of my uncle's abuse. She had caught him with me one day and brought me to confront my mother about her brother's perversion.

> *Mom abruptly slapped me across my mouth and called us both liars. My grandmother and mother screamed at each other, Grandma yelling, "God will punish you both," and mom yelling, "You liars. You go to hell." I sobbed, stricken from the blow and sure that I was responsible for my abuse and that God saw me as bad. To me, I was not worth God's love and as long as my uncle kept abusing me, I was a sinner and angered God.*

While he may not have doubted that Jesus was wronged, Thomas did doubt that Jesus had risen. Poole notes that we can learn something about doubting survivors by reading Thomas's story from the perspective of abuse.

After the resurrection, Jesus appears to a group of disciples, but Thomas is not with them. When the others tell Thomas about the risen Christ, he responds, "Unless I see the mark of the nails in his hands and put my finger in the mark of the nails and my hand in his side, I will not believe" (John 20:25).

Thomas doubts Jesus has risen from the dead. He won't believe unless he physically sees the risen Jesus. Similarly, we doubt sexual abuse survivors. We demand proof, just like Thomas. Poole points out just how invasive and coercive Thomas's demand is—he will not believe until he puts his fingers into the wounds on Jesus's hands and his hand into the wound in his side. Thomas demands to invade the very body that has been injured by torture and murder. His demand is not unlike the demands people often make of survivors to expose their wounds, to be retraumatized by intrusive examinations and questioning.[10] Doubt, then, becomes another kind of assault upon a victim.

We've seen this play out time and time again when survivors have come forward. As we mentioned in chapter 1, when Christine Blasey Ford testified that Supreme Court nominee Brett Kavanaugh had assaulted her when they were teens, many people disbelieved her.

Her clear memory of what happened to her as a teenager couldn't be accepted as the truth. She was scorned by strangers who thought that she was making up the story just to get attention. We've seen incredible denial by the Catholic Church in its clergy-abuse scandal. Again and again, the church has ignored complaints about predatory priests or simply moved them from diocese to diocese without warning. Now, many evangelicals are rushing to defend ministers accused of sexual abuse. The report of the investigation into Southern Baptists' handling of clergy abuse concluded that "survivors and others who reported abuse were ignored, disbelieved, or met with the constant refrain that the SBC could take no action."[11] Women in Grace Community Church, a California megachurch led by influential evangelical pastor John MacArthur, were even disciplined by the church for leaving men who abused them and their children. They demanded to see physical evidence of abuse or have a conviction for child sexual abuse before agreeing that women could leave their husbands.

Like Thomas, many people can't or won't wrap their minds around sexual abuse. Instead, they continue the violation by demanding people tell and retell their traumatic stories, provide physical proof, or set ridiculous standards for response like a criminal conviction. They deny, minimize, and cover up abuse and blame victims for what has happened. We find many doubting Thomases in the church when it comes to sexual abuse, and these doubting Thomases perpetuate the trauma of abuse.

Grace: Traumatic memories of sexual abuse and assault have a clear place within our own memories. Even though we may have never shared them with anyone, they are still embedded in our memories for a lifetime. This is true for me. I carry my own memories of sexual assault into middle age. These are clear and vivid memories which, if I share, people may doubt rather than believe me. People do not want to believe that their loved ones, their sister, their daughter, their aunt, or their mother could have been sexually abused. This is difficult to accept within their frame and scope of life. Therefore, much doubt can occur. And since sexual abuse and assault are taboo topics within Korean immigrant families, even if the victims speak up, they may be doubted.

Jo: I was at a Jesuit seminary studying theology, and there were all these paradigms about social justice and teaching and making the world a better place, but people couldn't hold the complexity of my pain. And it was like you're totally OK with like devoting your life to this as long as it's theoretical—like as long as it's in the classroom. But I'm coming to you as a friend with no support after remembering years of sexual violence against me in my family that was then covered up or justified under abusive Catholic ideology, and your response is to kind of stiff-arm me. That felt really hypocritical, and I think that was one of the reasons I also chose to leave the church. I was like, no. I'm just going to vote with my feet and liberate myself and go find love elsewhere. I don't believe love is something I should have to fight for—or safety. It was amazing leaving the church—it's so insular—and you think that's your whole world, and as soon as you leave, nobody cares about the Catholic Church. It was wild and similar with my family. You get on the other side of it and you're just like, there's a whole big world out there.

Surviving with Jesus

The story of Jesus doesn't end with his torture, sexual assault, and murder. Instead, the story surprises us with an unexpected turn of events. God resurrects Jesus from the dead.

The resurrection is God's affirmation of Jesus's decision to use love instead of power and to demand justice for the most marginalized. The resurrection tells us that Jesus is right all along, and God confirms Jesus's understanding of his role as struggling for love, peace, and justice rather than power. The resurrection is not an affirmation of power-over, hierarchy, and domination; rather, in the resurrection, God validates the poor, the meek, the outcast, the weak. The resurrection is God's demonstration of God's welcome and embrace for all of those who have been abused, tortured, traumatized, and violated.

Jesus's resurrection is hopeful for survivors of sexual abuse because we see that God affirms Jesus as a survivor, and, if God affirms Jesus, God affirms us as survivors as well. The crucifixion leaves us utterly hopeless. What more can we imagine beyond such awful cruelty, torment, and death? Many survivors certainly feel this way. Abuse is a kind of soul-murder, a destruction of our very being, and that annihilation of our sense of self causes deeper and longer suffering than the physical aspects of our abuse. We can spend years in therapy, practice yoga, meditate, pray, and still always the abuse will be with us. The hope of the resurrection is that we can use these tools to work through the debilitating effects of abuse to live again, beyond our abuse, that we can somehow integrate our abused selves into a fuller sense of self, a resurrected self.

Resurrection doesn't take our abuse away. It doesn't lessen or negate our suffering as victims. In Jesus's case, his resurrection doesn't diminish or nullify the suffering of torture, sexual assault, or the cross. Even after the resurrection, remember, Jesus's scars didn't go away.

Our hope isn't that we can forget our abuse or pretend it never happened. It's also not hope for the sweet by-and-by. It's a hope that we, like Jesus, can learn to live with our abuse, come to terms with its injustice, commit ourselves to living in love and justice, and thrive. It's a present resurrection, a resurrection that says that in this very moment, in the here and now, God affirms us as survivors. The *han* of our abuse is overcome in the love, acceptance, and welcome of God.

We have to be realistic about resurrection. Even Jesus, after his resurrection, told Mary, "Don't touch me." The scars are real. We don't know what Jesus thinks about his abuse. We don't know if sometimes he has nightmares where he's back in the Roman praetorium or hanging naked on the cross. We don't know if the sight of soldiers triggers him or if he sometimes feels that catch of anxiety and panic in his chest. Even resurrection doesn't change what happened to him—or to us. The hope of the resurrection is that suffering can be transformed into new life, a new life that absorbs and remakes suffering into love for all the world, a drive for justice, kindness, and peace.

This resurrection is present and ongoing. It doesn't happen all at once, and it's never fully complete. But it's also not a hope deferred until some idealized future after death. Jesus's resurrection is hope for us in the here and now. Because God affirmed the abused Jesus, we can know that God affirms our abused, suffering, and broken selves and the abused, suffering, and broken selves of all people.

The hope of resurrection is not some form of aspiration or a feeling of optimism. Rather, this hope is an urge and a desire that pushes us to work in love and toward social justice. We don't just resign ourselves to misery and hopelessness. Rather we resolve to work for justice. This is what hope is. The end goal of resurrection is never resurrection for its own sake. Personal salvation is never just that. Our redemption is always about all of us. To be resurrected is to work in the world to bring about God's in-breaking community.

We survive with Jesus by continuing Jesus's work in the world. Knowing God has affirmed us through Jesus's resurrection, we learn to embrace ourselves and to affirm ourselves by our work to bring about the world Jesus envisioned. Survival is personal; it's also political. We suffer sexual abuse because systems of oppression enable abuse and maintain themselves through abuse. Surviving abuse, then, is a political act. We resist the destruction of oppressive systems by surviving. But that's not enough. We also have to work to transform these systems so we can end sexual abuse. Our surviving personally is coupled with our helping others survive—from the ways we vote and donate, to the media we consume, to the causes for which we volunteer.

Jesus has shown us another way than the way of power, hierarchy, and violence. For Jesus, the way of God is the way of feeding the hungry, clothing the naked, helping the stranger in a ditch, and demanding equity and justice, whether from judges, religious leaders, or politicians. Surviving with Jesus can redirect our anger, our *han*, our despair. We can learn to accept ourselves, and we can work to create a better world. Things won't just be hunky-dory. Transformation is a process. The accurate language for faith is not that "we are saved" but that we are "being saved." Susan once heard poet Maya Angelou tell the story of a young man who asked her if she were "saved." "Are you?" Angelou responded. "Yes," he replied. "Really?" she countered, "Already?" Transformation is a process—and for survivors, it's a process with its ups and downs, flashbacks, and panic attacks. But, as the resurrection confirms, it is the better way; it is God's way.

Surviving with Jesus gives us hope that a different kind of world is possible—a world without sexual abuse, without misogyny and racism, and without violence. That's a world worth surviving for and working toward with faith that in each of us God truly is making all things new.

CHAPTER 9

Surviving with Joy

We are created for joy. Joy is the experience of being fully present in each moment, mindful of all the wonder it holds, attentive to our senses and the people and world around us. Suffering, especially the suffering that comes with abuse, prevents joy. Abuse can split survivors off from ourselves, especially from our bodies. Many of us who have survived abuse learned to dissociate as a way to survive. Susan still says she's the queen of dissociation, drawing on it now as a life skill when she needs it. But if we live constantly dissociated from our bodies and our emotions, we miss out on all of the possibilities of joy. Joy requires us to be fully present.

Episcopal priest Matthew Fox writes about ecstasy.[1] In fact, he says our ecstasies are experiences of God. He used to be a Catholic priest, but saying things like this got him defrocked, especially since he included sexual ecstasy as one of his examples. But he's right. He says ecstasies are those experiences when we're so deeply engaged in what's happening that we forget ourselves, we lose our self-consciousness, and therefore we are most nearly our true selves in these moments.

Black lesbian feminist Audre Lorde points us toward the erotic as a source of power.[2] For her, the erotic in our culture has become separated from everything but sex, but she says that, in reality, the erotic is the intensely felt joy we share when we are deeply engaged with others, particularly in the work of social justice. Patriarchy splits us off from the erotic by causing us to deny what we feel, through both our emotions and our bodies.

When Susan teaches this in her classes, she asks if a student is willing to come in front of the class and hug her twice. The first hug is a typical hug between two friends. The physical contact is mostly shoulders and above, with a significant amount of space between the rest of the two bodies. After that, she asks the student for a full body hug. Then she turns to the class and asks which one they think feels better. They always respond that the full body hug does. Susan then asks why they think we don't always give full body hugs since those feel better. One part of the conversation becomes about lesbian-baiting for women. Lesbian-baiting is using fear of being called a lesbian to control women's behavior. We keep women from feeling what they feel with other women by making them afraid. The second part of the conversation is about how culture has taught us to read bodily pleasure as always about wanting to have sex with someone. So, if a hug creates certain sensations, we learn to understand those as a desire to have sex. So, we don't do things that feel good if they might create those sensations. What if, however, we just learned to experience those wonderful sensations as pleasurable—even sexual pleasure—and understand that it doesn't mean we want to have sex with somebody. What if we could just feel what we feel and enjoy it? By making the erotic and sex the same thing, patriarchy ruptures possibilities for pleasure, intimacy, connection, and relational power.

For survivors of sexual abuse, the mind-body-emotion-spirit wiring has often been really messed up, and so feeling what we feel, especially when it involves bodies, can be terrifying. We learn to associate that electrical zing that makes our toes tingle with danger; a hand on the forearm can make us cringe; standing too close sends us into dissociation. It often takes us a long time to learn how to accept touching and to allow ourselves to feel pleasure in it, whether that touching is with a sexual partner or not.

Furthermore, Greco-Roman dualism, which heavily influenced early church doctrine and continues to impact the church today, didn't help us appreciate and love our own bodies. Dualism separates the body from spirit and claims that the body is sinful and bad while the spirit is good. This separation between the body and spirit creates a disconnect within us as we are taught that we should not enjoy bodily pleasure but only spiritual pleasure. This dualistic view of the world continues to affect the church today and has had a negative bearing on how to deal with sexual abuse. Dualism produces negative attitudes toward sexual abuse victims as they are often blamed or shamed for their own abuse. This negative attitude hinders healing from sexual abuse because survivors worry that, if they speak out, they may be labeled as sinners. Thus, many abuse victims internalize their abuse and do not seek help. Rather they just focus on spiritual care of the soul and spirit and not the body. They try to read the Bible, sing praise songs, and pray themselves to health, and they don't attend to the connections between soul wounds and body trauma.

This dualism also furthers patriarchy because it associates women (and feminized others) with the body and men with the mind/spirit. This becomes yet another argument for women's submission and oppression, confirming that women are less godlike because of their association with the body. This split then discourages victims of abuse from dealing holistically with their abuse. In fact, many evangelicals are now promoting biblical counseling, which argues that all the answers for psychological distress and its manifestations in the body (sleeplessness, depression, loss of appetite, illness, etc.) are in the Bible. Counselors don't need training in psychology, social work, or trauma. They just need to know the right Bible verses to quote and apply. This approach is dangerous for survivors of abuse who need support from people who understand the psychological, physical, emotional, relational, and spiritual consequences of sexual violence.

While the Bible certainly can be helpful, it is not a book of psychology, and, often in the church's hands, the Bible has done survivors more harm than good when they've been blamed for their own abuse, forced to forgive perpetrators, and told they just need to pray and believe more to be healed. But the truth is that survivors cannot pray the trauma away. We know from experience because we both tried.

> *Grace: I was told from an early age to focus on my personal piety, such as prayer, fasting, and reading the Bible. I was taught that my body was just a shell and unimportant. It is the spiritual side of me that was the essential part of who I am. Therefore, anything that happened to my body was not crucial. As a result, I viewed my abuse as unimportant even though the agony, pain, and grief were ever-present in my life. I was taught in the church that as long as my spirit is good, then I don't need to worry about anything else, including my own body. There was such a huge disconnect that all I could do to survive was just bury my sorrow deeper and deeper inside me until I couldn't hold it down any longer. When I finally sought help for my sexual abuse, I was in enormous agony. This led to a torrential rain of anguish, anger, and torment.*
>
> *It is long overdue for the church to break away from dualism. The Greco-Roman influence from over two thousand years ago has been detrimental to us and has been so harmful to sexual abuse victims and survivors. The church needs to teach that the body is good and that we need to take care of our bodies and understand how beautiful the body is. We need to treat our bodies as holy.*

The church doesn't help with all of its hang-ups about sexuality. Purity culture, in particular, has been devastating for many people, especially survivors. Even before their abuse, many survivors had already been taught that their bodies were sites of evil to be controlled at all costs. Susan once had a student who was convinced that even the briefest sexual thought was sin and required immediate repentance. Add these teachings to sexual violation, and survivors can be left with guilt, depression, dissociation, and despair. Being in your body is really hard when your body is the source of your pain and anger, the place that let you down by being vulnerable to a predator.

Susan: Early in life, I learned to distrust my body. After all, I couldn't even control it. I could, however, control my mind, and so that's where I went. Is it any wonder I'm an academic? I was incredibly uncomfortable in my body. I was ashamed of my body. To this day, I am only ever naked for as short a time as possible, even when I'm home alone. It's not about how my body looks, although it's certainly showing the effects of gravity and aging. My body just feels too vulnerable naked, too unsafe. It has taken me a long time to learn to be in my body. Frankly, the thing that has helped the most was becoming a feminist. Feminism values the body and sexuality, and the more I learned, the more I started to work on myself. I made a commitment to try to be in my body and to let myself feel what I feel. Other things helped too. Falling in love and coming out. (Of course, I'd also been taught shame about lesbian sexuality.) Getting my heart broken—twice—and working through it instead of running away from it. Marrying the love of my life. Reading Matthew Fox, Audre Lorde, Annie Dillard, and Thich Nhat Hanh, who helped me discover the discipline of mindfulness in various ways. Opening myself up to experiences of God at the Oregon coast, in dark chocolate, in the backbeat of classic rock, and in the passion of freely chosen sex. And practice at attentiveness. Lots and lots of practice. Finding joy is both a gift and a discipline. It can come upon us at any time, but it helps if we're looking for it and are aware of it when it's happening. So, I seek joy, whether in the taste of a fresh-picked strawberry out of my garden or in the new sights, sounds, and tastes of international travel, or in holding Catherine's hand, or in standing in solidarity at a protest. I am a seeker of joy in every moment, and that has transformed my life.

Grace: As a child, I never liked my body. First there was the horrible racism that I experienced in public school, where the kids made fun of my Asian features. Therefore, I was always ashamed of how I looked, and I just wanted to look like the rest of the white girls at school. But when the sexual assaults occurred, I came to detest my body even more. It was the site of fear, aggression, assault, and shame. Therefore, the hatred toward my body grew.

At church, they kept teaching and preaching to me about the importance of our spirit and that our bodies were unimportant. The body was evil, and it was the spirit that will live on forever in heaven. It was later, when I got married and had three children, that I realized that the body cannot be all that bad if it can miraculously produce another human being. I came to view my body as a holy place for miracles to happen and where life can begin and grow. The body became a place where love can be experienced and shared. The body also became a place where I can gain hope. Hope is not an optimistic feeling, but hope is like an anchor that can help hold us steady. Hope is from God and is a call to action even when things are bad. Hope is the power to help us work toward social justice. Hope helps us get to tomorrow. Through hope we can experience grace from all the harshness and pain from an abusive past. Hope brings forth joy and helps us know our bodies can be a place of happiness and joy. We all need to reclaim it as such.

The kind of joy we're talking about isn't some surface-level faux happiness that we're obligated to show because Jesus is the answer, no matter the question. It's much deeper than that and more real. It's a joy that lives side by side with trauma, grief, and anger. It's a both/and—both joy and grief, both joy and rage. And when joy takes grief and rage seriously, it is able to integrate them into a whole life, one where the body and emotions are not cut off from the mind. Joy is holistic; it holds body, emotion, and mind together in a unified experience of healing and well-being.

Surviving abuse can often feel like wandering in the wilderness. The ancient Hebrews wandered in the wilderness for forty years. Forty years of wandering! Forty years of manna day in and day out. Forty years of Moses. Forty years of grumbling.

Forty years of dry, boring, unending wilderness. Jesus spent forty days and nights in the desert, fasting and praying and wrestling with what kind of messiah he was going to be. But the wilderness is also a place where transformation takes place. When Jesus left the desert, Luke tells us, he was filled with the power of the Spirit and returned to Galilee. A report about him spread through all the surrounding country, and he began to teach in their synagogues and was praised by everyone (Luke 4:1–140). Jesus held on through the wilderness because he was onto something more than being stuck in the wilderness. Hagar also knew something about the wilderness. She ended up there twice! Each time, God came to her, and she named God there for herself. She liberated herself, and she became the mother of nations. We can find clarity in the wilderness, and the wilderness can sharpen our senses for detecting gaslighting, lies, and mistreatment. It can also prepare us for joy.

When Susan was a younger professor, she played a game with her students that involved running, smacking one another with Styrofoam "swords," and tackling (at sixty-two, when simply rolling over in the bed can cause grievous injury, Susan does not play this game anymore). As the group played, there was lots of competition, physical contact (and students could always opt out and become observers only), and raucous laughter. No one was thinking about anything but the game. Self-consciousness disappeared. So did worry about anything else. Only that moment existed for all the players. They were fully in their bodies because they were not thinking about how they looked or what anyone else was thinking about them. They were simply fully and completely in the moment. It was pure joy. It was an experience of God shared by the group who, after the game, talked about what happened, laughing, learning, loving one another, nursing an occasional bruise, and feeling God in their midst.

As Susan said, joy is both a gift and a discipline. Sometimes it comes upon us when we are not expecting it at all—a shaft of sunlight falling on the first spring crocus, your favorite song blasting out of the car stereo, ocean waves crashing on rocks, finishing that thing you thought you could not do. Joy can come upon us unexpectedly; it can wash over us, enfold us, fill us, overwhelm us with feelings too ancient and deep to name. It becomes the unexpected grace that fills our souls with peace and love.

And joy is also a discipline. We seek it; we hunger and thirst after it; we practice it until it becomes habit. How? By directing our attention at every moment to even the smallest of objects, sensations, and emotions in our path. We have to teach ourselves to look for it until our looking becomes habituated. For example, look at your hand. Have you ever marveled at it? Look at everything it can do. Now look deeper. In your mind's eye, look at the atoms that make up your hand. Every single particle in your hand has existed from the time of the Big Bang. These particles have been other things—perhaps a star, a meteor, a wildflower—and, when your body returns to the earth, these particles will continue to exist and become other things forever and ever. Doesn't that make you want to shout "hallelujah" to the end of your days?

Everything alive vibrates. Everything in the universe is vibrating right now. The atoms are in constant motion even though things look static. Atoms are always moving and vibrating. When we think about the Spirit of God, the Spirit is vibration. The Spirit as vibration fills our bodies, the earth, and the whole universe. Light, sound, and everything alive are vibrating. It is the Spirit of God as vibration which fills us with joy and gives us life and goodness. It is a joy which comes like a crashing wave and also a joy that comes so silently that it just nudges us and moves us forward toward wholeness. Joy is what sustains us in life. Even after the most difficult times, hardships, abuse, and assaults that we may undergo, we can overcome these traumatic events by the Spirit of God which vibrates in us and produces joy.

Think of a time when you've seen something so beautiful words could not begin to express your feelings—a meteor shower on a cloudless night or the Grand Tetons on a clear blue day, your new baby or grandbaby, a blanket of snow, or a rainbow across the sky. Have you been filled with wonder at the fact that the world is such that light can bounce into your eyes from an object, your brain can perceive it as beauty, and your whole being can be filled with emotion at what you perceive?

Practicing joy asks us to be mindful to look for these things. When you eat, stop and notice the colors, smells, textures of your food. Savor the taste. Remember with gratitude all the people who were involved in getting that food to your table.

Do the things you love most with purpose, looking for joy. Take a picnic to a park. Pay attention to what you pack. Think about each item, its color, texture, smell, and taste. Pick a perfect spot for you. Susan and Catherine bought themselves really nice camping chairs that stay in the car all summer for just this purpose. When they hike, they find a perfect spot for a picnic lunch, pull out the chairs, and set up with their picnic backpack, cooler, and all of their favorite picnic items—bread, cheese, nuts, olives, grapes . . . and Cheetos. Pay attention to what you eat. Savor each bite. Look around you and take in everything around you—the sky, the land, the plants, the birds, the people. Breathe deeply, mindfully. Thich Nhat Hanh suggests we breathe in through our noses, repeating, "Breathing in, I calm myself," then breathing out through our mouths and saying, "Breathing out I smile."[3]

Be in your body. Joy is a sensual experience as well as an emotional and spiritual one. Feel the strain of your muscles as you move, take in the colors, notice the smells, listen for the slightest whispers. Embrace it all and rejoice in it. When Susan and Catherine picnic, inevitably one of them says to the other, "This is the life!" The other one says back, "Yes, it is!"

This is joy, ecstasy, and experience of God. For survivors, these moments can remind us of the good in the world and, even if only for the briefest of moments, can intervene in our grief and anger. Practiced across a lifetime, joy may become a way of living for some.

That's not to say struggle ends or that all survivors can or must reach this place. We recognize the long-lasting impacts of trauma, and we believe that survivors deserve to live in joy. We believe that joy is what God desires for all of us, and we also know that struggle with trauma is a lifetime reality. Part of the *han* of sexual abuse is that, no matter what, those scars and memories will always be with us. Our hope, for all survivors, however, is that reimagining God as we have and accepting experiences of joy as experiences of God can help mitigate some of the pain of abuse and help survivors envision another way forward.

Sexual abuse, as we've discussed, can make us feel that God has abandoned us or punished us, especially when our churches are telling us that God controls everything. If we conceive of God as persuasive love rather than coercive power, then we can recognize that God does not will, allow, or want our abuse and our suffering. Our abuse happens because someone with physical, emotional, psychological, institutional, or spiritual power over us makes a choice to do harm to us. God calls people to do what is good and just and loving, but people can choose to do what is evil and oppressive and hateful. When they do, God suffers with us in our suffering. God with us cries out for justice. God holds us in God's embrace, even when we may not feel it, and God comes to us in joy.

Susan: Looking back now I can see that even during the years of my abuse God was with me. Books brought me great joy, and I read voraciously. At the time, I didn't understand that as God with me, but now I do. That great joy helped me survive. I experienced joy when my friend Kathy played her guitar and sang. Listening to Linda Ronstadt albums gave me joy. My youth group at church gave me joy. I wish back then I had known this was where God was. I thought God was in my guilt and self-blame, that God judged me as harshly as I did. I'm reminded of Elijah. As he stood on the mountain waiting, there came a great wind, then an earthquake, and then a fire. But God was not in the wind or the earthquake or the fire. After those came a still, small voice. For me, God was not in the sermons or the Sunday school lessons or the guilt or the good Christian man who abused me. No. God was in the books, the friends, the music. I see that now.

Grace: Growing up in the church and attending different denominational churches, I believed that God was loud and that we also needed to be loud in our prayers, in our faith, and in our love for God. But when the abuse happened and God was silent, I felt that God was not with me. I thought that God had abandoned me as I was tarnished goods and not worthy of God's love. I really believed that God became distant and could not be present with me and could not love a broken girl. During these difficult times, I felt alone, discarded, and unworthy. During these most trying times, I turned to reading books.

My parents didn't have much money, so we had hardly any books at home. Books were not essential items like food and clothing. Therefore, I borrowed books from the library. The books became a place where I could escape from personal pain and anguish. The books became a place where I could experience some sort of joy in my life. It was not in the loud Pentecostal revival services that I experienced God, but, rather, I experienced God elsewhere and differently. God was present in the stillness, the quietness, and the solitude. In those instances, I knew that God was nearby and was still loving me despite my brokenness.

If we open our minds and hearts and bodies, we can realize that all our experiences of joy are experiences of God. God is present in our joy. God enjoys our joy. God comes to us in our joy, whether in watching basketball or singing in the choir or having a baby or reading books or eating Cheetos on a picnic after a hike in the Oregon Coast Range. God desires joy for us, in the here and now.[4]

Rock City is a tourist attraction atop Lookout Mountain in north Georgia. It's most known for its "Lover's Leap" rock, its site where you can see seven states, and its Fairyland Caverns with sculpted and lit fairytale scenes. Starting in 1935, the attraction's founder paid farmers around the area to paint their barn roofs black with bold white lettering urging "See Rock City." Susan's friend musician Kate Campbell wrote a song about a woman in Mississippi who decides that it's time to live a little. For too long, she's worked her monotonous days in her mama's beauty shop, and now she wants to find herself and her place in the world. And so, she throws a map and a tube of lipstick into an old Winn Dixie sack, pulls her Firebird out of the driveway, and heads out—to see Rock City—before it gets too late.[5]

In the song, Rock City is a metaphor for those unrealized dreams we have that are only beyond our grasp because we fail to reach for them. Rock City is the chance for the life we truly desire, not just the life we live because we happen to have fallen into it. But, to get to Rock City, we must get in our Firebirds and drive. To live in joy, we have to reach for it, to pay attention, to risk opening our abused and traumatized hearts to feel it.

In the Bible, we learn that a woman named Ruth had married the son of Naomi. Naomi and her family were immigrants in Moab during a famine in Israel. While in Moab, Naomi's husband and sons died, and she decided to return to her hometown. When she set out, both of her daughters-in-law were with her, but Naomi convinced one of them to return to her own family. Ruth, on the other hand, was determined to follow her heart, no matter what Naomi said. Listen to Ruth's response to Naomi: "Do not press me to leave you or to turn back from following you! Where you go, I will go; Where you lodge, I will lodge; your people shall be my people, and your

God my God. Where you die, I will die—and there be buried.
May the Lord do thus and so to me, and more as well, if even
death parts me from you" (Ruth 1:16–17). Ruth had lost everything, but she took the risk to follow her heart.

Of course, following your heart has a certain element of
risk to it, and there's always a price to pay. Ruth was a young,
widowed woman. Most often, women in her position ended
up in prostitution in order to support themselves. She was
choosing to travel with an older widowed woman. What kind
of assurance was that! And she was moving to another country
where people were not always especially receptive to foreigners.

What do you think would have happened to Ruth if she had
turned back? Would she have spent the rest of her days longing
for her mother-in-law, missing the intimacy of that relationship, wondering what might have been? We think of Simon
Peter, who so brashly jumped off the boat to walk with Jesus on
the water. After only a couple of steps, he saw the waves around
him and got scared, and he began to sink. While some may
hear this story and think of Peter as a dismal failure, we hear
this story and see the only disciple who actually even stepped
out of the boat. It may have only been a couple of steps on the
water, but that's a couple more steps than the other disciples
made—and oh, what glorious steps those must have been!

Of course, there are still suffering and injustice in the world,
and survivors often still suffer and experience injustice, and we
hold all of this in our present moment as well. We know risk is
real, and yet risk is our only path to joy. Our joy then compels
us to remove as much suffering and injustice from the world
as we can. This is how we work with God to bring in God's
community. And here is where liberation theologies become
useful for survivors.

Sexual abuse isn't simply a problem between individual
people. Rather, it is a symptom of the system of patriarchy,
shaped by racism, heterosexism, ableism, classism, ageism,

and other systems of oppression. Intersectional theology helps us see the interconnectedness and entanglement of the many forms of oppression. The different systems of oppression reinforce each other to create new categories of suffering. For example, Grace is not just a woman, but a woman of color and an immigrant. Hence Grace faces oppression at the intersection of race and gender. The different identities of Grace illustrate that there are no single-issue struggles but rather multi-issue struggles. Furthermore, there is an interconnectedness of many oppressions, such as ageism, homophobia, sexism, racism, and ableism which intertwine together to oppress. These forms of oppressions are interrelated and thrive off the same economic and social powers in which straight, white, able-bodied men are the norm against which all others are defined. Recognizing this and fighting all these forms of oppression is crucial to our survival and movement toward healing and joy.

Liberation theologies help us see our individual experiences as part of these larger systems that maintain and reproduce oppression. They help us see that we're not alone in what has happened to us and that more is at work than meets the eye. The interlocking systems of economic injustice, racial injustice, gender injustice, and so on continue to oppress individuals and communities. Liberation theologies seek new ways of experiencing freedom from these various intersecting oppressions so people will not feel subjugated, subordinated, or diminished due to sexual violence and gender injustice.

Within feminist liberation theologies, in particular, we are able to name the things that happened to us as abuse, as patriarchal (as well as racialized) violence, and as sin. Sin in liberation theologies is structural, and, for feminist theologians, sin is also gendered. Patriarchy uses sexual violence to keep women, children, and sexual minorities in their place. Feminist theologies name not only the individual things that happened to us as sin but also the structures that enabled and facilitated what happened to us as sin. For example, think about clergy abuse.

Certainly, we recognize the sinfulness of abusive acts toward women and children by clergy. Feminist theologies also help us understand how the patriarchal structures of churches help facilitate this sin by teaching submission, excluding women, and promoting purity culture. When we are able to name the structures, we give ourselves a place to make real change. For the Catholic Church, removing a few priests credibly accused of abuse and issuing statements will never end the problem of clergy abuse because the church's patriarchal structures remain intact. Similarly, Southern Baptists' plans to address their abuse scandal fall short because they do not challenge the root causes of clergy abuse.

Furthermore, Christianity's focus on piety looks at sin vertically and not horizontally. That's why repenting is more important than restitution. Sexual violence is a sin against God more so than a sin against another person. The disruption of a relationship with God is the real problem, not the violation of a relationship with another more vulnerable person. That's why the church can often ignore, deny, and cover up sexual abuse. The consequences of abuse on the victim are not an important part of the theological equation of the perpetrator's relationship with God or the importance of maintaining the institution of the church. From the perspectives of survivors, however, *han* reminds us of the other side of sin, the harm perpetrators cause their victims. Abuse is a sin against the victim, and so the church must center the victim in its response; like God, the church must side with the victim while calling the perpetrator to justice. The church must also be involved in the movement to end sexual violence and to facilitate justice for victims and perpetrators.

One of the healing things survivors can do is become involved in movements for social justice that confront and transform the structures that enable sexual violence. Because all of our struggles are linked, survivors can find joy and hope in working with people in other social justice movements, like the disability rights movement, the Black Lives Matter movement, the movement to end gun violence, or the prison abolition movement. Sexual violence is linked in some ways to all other kinds of violence, and people in other minoritized groups face violence or the threat of violence every day. All of our struggles are linked.

There is joy in the struggle for justice. Minister and writer Victoria Safford explains it this way:

> Our mission is to plant ourselves at the gates of hope—not the prudent gates of Optimism, which are somewhat narrower; nor the stalwart, boring gates of Common Sense; nor the strident gates of self-righteousness, which creak on shrill and angry hinges; nor the cheerful, flimsy garden gate of "Everything is gonna be all right," but a very different, sometimes very lonely place, the place of truth-telling, about your own soul first of all and its condition, the place of resistance and defiance, the piece of ground from which you see the world both as it is and as it could be, as it might be, as it will be; the place from which you glimpse not only struggle, but joy in the struggle—and we stand there, beckoning and calling, telling people what we are seeing, asking people what they see.[6]

Simply surviving abuse is a form of resistance, a labor in the struggle. Finding joy in the struggle is a triumph for survivors. Knowing what we have overcome simply by surviving beckons us to struggle joyfully alongside others who also survive their own hells and oppressions. The struggle is an experience of God because God is with us in the struggle, whether the struggle is against the traumatic harms done to us in our abuse or against racism in policing, trans exclusion, or anti-abortion legislation. God struggles with us.

Susan: I think as much as any group, queer folks have found joy in the struggle. I remember so well how it felt to go to my first

Pride parade. This was after the early protests and before so much commercialization of Pride. Coming out in my context as a religion professor in conservative Christian colleges had been difficult, to say the least. I finally quit, not knowing what was next, but it set me free. That first pride parade was sheer joy for me as I watched the Dykes on Bikes, the drag queens, the marching bands, the service organizations, and all the wonderful, sometimes wacky, queer folks walk by. I felt at home. These were my people. Sure, I'm not one to sport leather chaps and bare bottoms in public, but (no pun intended) these were my people. I felt love and connection to all of them and each of them. I felt powerful and seen. I felt sheer joy. Queer folks know how to party and struggle. After all, our bars and drag shows and bookstores and parades have always been sites for resistance and fun, tears and laughter, joy in struggle. God is there. On the floats and in the bands. In the bars and on the stage. In me and my colorful, defiant, loving queer community.

Struggle brings about change, slowly, haltingly, sometimes two steps forward and one step back. Struggle can help transform us as we turn our grief and anger toward something bigger to help ourselves and others. Struggle can also make structural change. Suffrage. Integrated schools. Title IX. The Americans with Disabilities Act. Marriage equality. Of course, structural transformation is no more complete than our personal transformation. There's more work to be done. If we attend to our senses, our bodies, our surroundings, our emotions, our relationships, we can find joy. We can find God.

Isn't it enough to send us all shouting "hallelujah" for the rest of our days? Joy to the world! And as Three Dog Night reminds us, "Joy to you and me."

Engaging process theology, intersectional theology, and liberation theologies from the perspectives of survivors of sexual violence shows us how we can name and critique what happened to us and how we can find joy in the struggle for justice for ourselves and others. Survivors show us the lie of the God who undergirds sexual abuse, violence, rape. Survivors show us another way, a way of the God who suffers with us, embraces us, empowers us, and accompanies us on the journey, the God who struggles for justice alongside us, the God who comes to us with joy in the midst of it all. This Surviving God has survived the perversions of God's nature advanced by many abusers and churches. This Surviving God has suffered and survived with us. This Surviving God struggles with us each step of the way for healing, justice, love, and joy. This Surviving God is in the joy we feel at the breeze on our cheeks and the cheesecake in the fridge, at the BLM protest and the fresh scent of clothes just out of the dryer, at the Indigo Girls concert when they sing "Closer to Fine" as the encore, and at church when the pastor reads that favorite passage that offers comfort and inspiration. Rethinking God from the perspectives of survivors means imagining a God who embraces us with all our complexities and contradictions, who suffers with us, who calls out with us for justice, and who wishes joy for each of us.

Surviving God is not an endpoint but a process, a little like the road to Hana on Maui. If you take the famous fifty-two-mile road with its 620 curves and fifty-nine bridges as fast you can to get to Hana, you can probably make it there in two hours, but you'll miss the point of the drive. Sure, Hana's a great little town, but it's the waterfalls and views and seascapes along the way that are the real gems of the journey. Surviving God has its own share of hairpin turns and harrowing drop-offs, and as we make our way we also encounter mercy and grace and love. Paul Simon sings a song called "Graceland." There's a verse that goes: "There is a girl in New York City / Who calls herself the human trampoline / And sometimes when I'm falling, flying / Or tumbling in turmoil I say / 'Whoa, so this is what she means.' / She means we're bouncing into Graceland."[7] Surviving God is a lot like that. Surviving God isn't an easy path, but it's a joyful one, even if it means we're bouncing into Graceland.

The grace of God is not simply a warm fuzzy we get when we go to church. The grace of God is an illumination of ourselves, a clear, honest, searing moment of self-recognition after which we will never be the same, seeing ourselves as we truly are, and then knowing that this self we try to hide, this real self, is embraced by the love of God which calls us to be more than we are. This truth is grace. This unmerited, boundless, constant outpouring of goodness no matter what. No matter what was done to us. No matter what we've done or what has happened to us since. No matter how often we fall short. No matter how many times we forget the words or get our choir robes tucked into our pantyhose. It is grace because we can bounce into it.

There is no one way to survive, and surviving is never easy, but we can be assured that we are held in the loving embrace of the God who walks alongside us, suffers and rejoices with us, demands justice in the world, and calls us to be God's people of love and justice. Because God survives with us, we know we stand a chance against the trauma and against the systems of misogyny, racism, ableism, homo- and transphobia, and ageism that beset us. Nothing—not sexual abuse, not bad theology, not cover-ups, nor denials—can separate us from the love of God. That's good news we can hold onto as we're bouncing along.

Acknowledgments

There is always a wonderful community behind every book. We are incredibly grateful to all the survivors who spoke with us and shared their experiences and perspectives: Jo Lauren, Dawn Schiller, David Pittman, Janet, Shannon, Sara, Laura, Christa, and all the unnamed survivors whose words have helped us construct a new vision of God through the eyes of survivors of sexual abuse.

We're really glad our Broadleaf editor Lisa Kloskin believed in our idea for the book and our ability to write it, and we appreciate her work behind the scenes to bring this project to fruition. We also appreciate the keen editing eye of Janet Lockhart, who helped two academics be sure not to sound like we're giving a class lecture.

We're both very grateful to our spouses, Perry Lee and Catherine Draper, and family, who put up with our hours at our computers and away from time with family. We also appreciate their support as we've dredged up some of the most painful parts of our pasts and worked day after day with this difficult material. Grace is also thankful to her children, Theo, Elisabeth, and Joshua, for their moral support. We're so glad they all love us and cheer us on whenever we come up with a new project idea.

Notes

Preface

1 Toinette M. Eugene, "'Swing Low, Sweet Chariot!': A Womanist Ethical Response to Sexual Violence and Abuse," in *Violence Against Women and Children: A Christian Theological Sourcebook*, ed. Carol J. Adams and Marie M. Fortune (New York: Continuum, 1995), 185–200.

2 United States Conference of Catholic Bishops, "Created Male and Female: An Open Letter from Religious Leaders," December 15, 2017, http://www.usccb.org/issues-and-action/marriage-and-family/marriage/promotion-and-defense-of-marriage/created-male-and-female.cfm.

Chapter 1

1 Marcella Althaus-Reid, *Indecent Theology: Theological Perspectives in Sex, Gender and Politics* (New York: Routledge, 2001), 2.

2 Audre Lorde, *The Cancer Journals*, 2nd ed. (San Francisco: Aunt Lute, 1980), 20.

3 Sandra Newman, "What Kind of Person Makes False Rape Accusations?" *Quartz*, May 11, 2017, https://qz.com/980766/the-truth-about-false-rape-accusations/.

4 "The Women Killed on One Day around the World," BBC News (website), November 25, 2018, https://www.bbc.com/news/world-46292919.

5 For more statistics on gender-based violence, see the 2018 report by Stop Street Harassment, "The Facts behind the #MeToo Movement: A National Study on Sexual Harassment and Assault," Stop Street Harassment, February 2018, http://www.stopstreetharassment.org/wp-content/uploads/2018/01/Full-Report-2018-National-Study-on-Sexual-Harassment-and-Assault.pdf.

6 "Why Nearly All Mass Shooters Are Men," NPR, March 27, 2021, https://www.npr.org/2021/03/27/981803154/why-nearly-all-mass-shooters-are-men.

7 "Elliot Rodger: How Misogynist Killer Became 'Incel Hero,'" BBC News (website), April 26, 2018, https://www.bbc.com/news/world-us-canada-43892189.

8 Kimberlé Williams Crenshaw and Andrea J. Ritchie, with Rachel Anspach, Rachel Gilmer, and Luke Harris, "Say Her Name: Resisting Police Brutality against Black Women," African American Policy Forum, 2015, https://static1.squarespace.com/static/53f20d90e4b0b80451158d8c/t/5edc95fba357687217b08fb8/1591514635487/SHNReportJuly2015.pdf.

9 Kelly Brown Douglas, *Stand Your Ground: Black Bodies and the Justice of God* (Maryknoll, NY: Orbis Books, 2015).

Chapter 2

1 Sallie McFague, *Speaking in Parables: A Study in Metaphor and Theology* (Minneapolis: Fortress Press, 1975), 4.

2 McFague, *Speaking in Parables*, 4.

3 Alfred North Whitehead, *Science and the Modern World* (New York: The New American Library, 1925), 52.

4 Grace Ji-Sun Kim and Susan M. Shaw, *Intersectional Theology: An Introductory Guide* (Minneapolis: Fortress Press, 2019).

5 Sallie McFague, *Models of God: Theology for an Ecological Nuclear Age* (Minneapolis: Fortress Press, 1987).

6 Mercy Amba Oduyoye, "The African Experience of God through the Eyes of an Akan Woman," *Cross Currents* 47, no. 4 (Winter 1997/98): 493–504, https://www.jstor.org/stable/24460601.

Chapter 3

1 Dietrich Bonhoeffer, *The Cost of Discipleship* (London: SCM Press, 1959), 4.

2 Kyle Swenson, "A Pastor Admitted a Past 'Sexual Incident' with a Teen, Saying He Was 'Deeply Sorry.' His Congregation Gave Him a Standing Ovation," *Washington Post*, January 10, 2018.

3 Lauren Effron, Andrew Paparella, and Jeca Taudte, "The Scandals That Brought Down the Bakkers, Once among US's Most Famous Televanglists," ABC News, December 20, 2019, https://abcnews.go.com/US/scandals-brought-bakkers-uss-famous-televangelists/story?id=60389342.

4 Bob Smietana, "Bible Teacher Beth Moore, Trump Critic and Advocate for Sexual Abuse Victims, Splits with Southern Baptist Convention," *Washington Post*, March 9, 2021.

5 "Southern Baptist Convention: Resolution on Ordination and the Role of Women in Ministry," June 1, 1984, https://www.sbc.net/resource-library/resolutions/resolution-on-ordination-and-the-role-of-women-in-ministry/.

6 Sarah Pulliam Bailey, "Southern Baptist Leader Who Advised Abused Women Not to Divorce Doubles Down, Says He Has Nothing to Apologize For," *Washington Post*, May 4, 2018.

7 Jeff Coen, "Claims against Willow Creek's Bill Hybels of 'Sexually Inappropriate' Conduct Are Credible, New Report Says," *Chicago Tribune*, February 28, 2019, https://www.chicagotribune.com/news/breaking/ct-met-willow-creek-church-bill-hybels-report-20190228-story.html.

8 Part of this section was initially published on the *Ms.* blog as "How Evangelical Theology Supports a Culture of Abuse," *Ms. Magazine* (blog), September 27, 2018, http://msmagazine.com/blog/2018/09/27/evangelical-theology-supports-culture-sexual-abuse/.

9 Robert Downen, Lise Olsen, and John Tedesco, "Abuse of Faith: 20 Years, 700 Victims: Southern Baptist Sexual Abuse Spreads as Leaders Resist Reform," *Houston Chronicle*, February 10, 2019.

10 "Report of the Independent Investigation: The Southern Baptist Convention Executive Committee's Response to Sexual Abuse Allegations and an Audit of the Procedures and Actions of the Credentials Committee," May 15, 2022. Washington, DC: Guidepost Solutions. https://static1.squarespace.com/static/6108172d83d55d3c9db4d-d67/t/628a9326312a4216a3c0679d/1653248810253/Guidepost+Solutions+Independent+Investigation+Report.pdf.

11 Ray Sanchez, "Famed Evangelist Ravi Zacharias Engaged in Sexual Misconduct, His Ministry Says," CNN, February 12, 2021.

12 "L'Arche Founder Jean Vanier Sexually Abused Women—Internal Report," BBC News (website), February 22, 2020, https://www.bbc.com/news/world-51596516.

13 Soli Salgado, "Allegations of Sexual Harassment against John Howard Yoder Extend to Notre Dame," *National Catholic Reporter*,

June 25, 2015, https://www.ncronline.org/news/accountability/allegations-sexual-harassment-against-john-howard-yoder-extend-notre-dame.

14   Mark Oppenheimer, "A Theologian's Influence, and Stained Past, Live On," *New York Times*, October 11, 2013, https://www.nytimes.com/2013/10/12/us/john-howard-yoders-dark-past-and-influence-lives-on-for-mennonites.html.

15   Andrew Prokop, "The Jerry Falwell Jr. Scandal, Explained," *Vox*, August 25, 2020, https://www.vox.com/2020/8/25/21399954/jerry-falwell-jr-resigns-scandal-liberty.

16   Derrick Bryson Taylor, "Carl Lentz, Pastor to Celebrities, Is Fired from Hillsong Church," *New York Times*, November 5, 2020, https://www.nytimes.com/2020/11/05/us/hillsong-carl-lentz-fired.html.

17   Author's notes, PANAWTM Meeting, New York City, spring 1998.

18   Elisabeth Schüssler Fiorenza, *In Memory of Her: A Feminist Theological Reconstruction of Christian Origins* (New York: Crossroad Publishing, 1990), 153.

19   "Measuring the #MeToo Backlash," *The Economist*, October 20, 2018, https://www.economist.com/united-states/2018/10/20/measuring-the-metoo-backlash.

Chapter 4

1   David Adams Leeming, *God: Myths of the Male Divine* (Oxford: Oxford University Press, 1997), 4.

2   Lisa Sharon Harper, *Fortune: How Race Broke My Family and the World and How to Repair It All* (Grand Rapids, MI: Brazos Press, 2022), 38.

3   John Donne, "Holy Sonnets: Batter My Heart, Three-Person'd God," accessed September 15, 2020, https://www.poetryfoundation.org/poems/44106/holy-sonnets-batter-my-heart-three-persond-god.

4   George Matheson, "Make Me a Captive, Lord," *Baptist Hymnal* (Nashville: Convention Press, 1991).

5   Mary Daly, *Beyond God the Father* (Boston: Beacon Press, 1985), 19.

6   James Newton Poling, *The Abuse of Power: A Theological Problem* (Nashville: Abingdon Press, 1991), 173.

7   Karen L. Bloomquist, "Sexual Violence: Patriarchy's Offense and Defense," in *Christianity, Patriarchy, and Abuse: A Feminist Critique*, ed. Joanne Carlson Brown and Carole R. Bohn (New York: Pilgrim Press, 1989), 67.

8   Joerg Rieger, *Jesus vs. Caesar: For People Tired of Serving the Wrong God* (Nashville: Abingdon Press, 2018), 39.

9 Poling, *The Abuse of Power*, 165.

10 Poling, 166.

11 Rita Nakashima Brock and Rebecca Ann Parker, *Proverbs of Ashes: Violence, Redemptive Suffering, and the Search for What Saves Us* (Boston: Beacon Press, 2001), 198.

12 Brock and Parker, *Proverbs of Ashes*, 156.

13 Brock and Parker, 156.

14 Rita Nakashima Brock, *Journeys by Heart: A Christology of Erotic Power* (New York: Crossroad Publishing, 1988), 56.

15 Brock and Parker, *Proverbs of Ashes*, 44.

16 James Cone, *The Cross and the Lynching Tree* (Maryknoll, NY: Orbis Books, 2011), xix.

17 Ewen MacAskill, "George Bush: 'God Told Me to End the Tyranny in Iraq,'" *The Guardian*, October 7, 2005, https://www.theguardian.com/world/2005/oct/07/iraq.usa.

18 Department of Defense Sexual Assault and Prevention Response Office, "SAPRO Report, Metrics Overview," accessed May 23, 2023, https://www.sapr.mil/sites/default/files/public/docs/reports/SAPRO_Report_Metrics_Overview_ReferenceCopy.pdf.

19 Rita Nakashima Brock, *Journeys by Heart* (Eugene, OR: Wipf & Stock, 2008), 51.

20 Brock, *Journeys by Heart*, 55.

21 Carrie Newcomer, "Betty's Diner," Regulars and Refugees, Rounder Records, 2005.

22 Barbara Kingsolver, *The Bean Trees* (New York: HarperTorch, 1988), 145.

Chapter 5

1 "The Dry Salvages," *The Four Quartets*, in *T.S. Eliot: The Complete Poems and Plays* (New York: Harcourt, Brace & World, 1971), 136.

2 Elizabeth A. Johnson, *Quest for the Living God: Mapping Frontiers in the Theology of God* (New York: Continuum, 2007), 56.

3 Poling, *The Abuse of Power*, 173.

4 Andrew Sung Park, *The Wounded Heart of God: The Asian Concept of Han and the Christian Doctrine of Sin* (Nashville: Abingdon Press, 1993), 121.

5 Rita Nakishima Brock, "And a Little Child Will Lead Us: Christology and Child Abuse," in *Christianity, Patriarchy, and Abuse: A Feminist Critique*, ed. Joanne Carlson Brown and Carole R. Bohn (New York: Pilgrim Press, 1989), 55.

6 Poling, *The Abuse of Power*, 174.

7   Jürgen Moltmann, *The Trinity and the Kingdom: The Doctrine of God* (Minneapolis: Fortress Press, 1991), 174.

8   Delores S. Williams, *Sisters in the Wilderness: The Challenge of Womanist God-Talk* (Maryknoll, NY: Orbis Books, 2013), xiii; Monica A. Coleman, *Making a Way Out of No Way: A Womanist Theology* (Minneapolis: Fortress Press, 2008).

9   Williams, *Sisters in the Wilderness*, xiv.

10 Karen Baker-Fletcher, *A Singing Something: Womanist Reflections on Anna Julia Cooper* (New York: Crossroads Press, 1994), 195.

11 Coleman, *Making a Way Out of No Way*, 33.

12 Coleman, 36.

13 Fairfax County Department of Family Services, "Sexual Violence Survivors at Greater Risk of Suicide," September and December 2020, https://www.fairfaxcounty.gov/familyservices/community-corner/sexual-violence-survivors-at-greater-risk-of-suicide.

14 Elizabeth A. Johnson, *She Who Is: The Mystery of God in Feminist Theological Discourse*, 3rd ed. (New York: Herder & Herder, 2017), 50.

15 Patrick Cheng, *Radical Love: Introduction to Queer Theology* (New York: Seabury Books, 2011).

Chapter 6

1   Phyllis Trible, *Texts of Terror: Literary-Feminist Readings of Biblical Narratives* (Philadelphia: Fortress Press, 1984).

2   Elisabeth Schüssler Fiorenza, *Bread Not Stone: The Challenge of Feminist Biblical Interpretation* (Boston: Beacon Press, 1984, 1995), 15–19.

3   Rhiannon Graybill, *Texts after Terror: Rape, Sexual Violence, & the Hebrew Bible* (New York: Oxford University Press, 2021), 12–17.

4   A note about language: We are using the language of "First Testament" and "Christian Testament" to refer to the two major parts of the Bible. This is in recognition that the First Testament is still the scripture of Judaism. "Old Testament" and "New Testament" suggest that the First Testament is no longer relevant and has been superseded by the Christian Testament. "First Testament" and "Christian Testament" recognize that both testaments are still the authoritative texts of two of the world's major religions.

5   Laura Sauder, "Sexual Property and the Personhood of Women in the Old Testament, New Testament and the Mishnah," *Consensus* 33, no. 2 (2011): 1, 2.

6 Sauder, "Sexual Property and the Personhood of Women in the Old Testament, New Testament and the Mishnah," 2.

7 Helen Schügnel-Straumann, "Genesis 1–11: The Primordial History," in *Feminist Biblical Interpretation: A Compendium of Critical Commentary on the Books of the Bible and Related Literature*, ed. Luise Schottroff and Marie-Theres Wacker, trans. Lisa E. Dahill et al. (Grand Rapids, MI: William B. Eerdmans, 2012), 1–14.

8 Schügnel-Straumann, "Genesis 1–11: The Primordial History."

9 Deryn Guest, *When Deborah Met Jael: Lesbian Biblical Hermeneutics* (London: SCM Press, 2005), 146.

10 Guest, *When Deborah Met Jael*, 150.

11 Graybill, *Texts after Terror*, 46.

12 Irmtraud Fischer, "Genesis 12–15: The Story of Israel's Origins as a Women's Story," in *Feminist Biblical Interpretation*, ed. Schottroff and Wacker, trans. Dahill et al., 15–32.

13 Wilda Gafney, *Womanist Midrash: A Reintroduction to the Women of the Torah and the Throne* (Louisville, KY: Westminster John Knox, 2017), 30.

14 Graybill, *Texts after Terror*, 45.

15 Randall Bailey, "They're Nothing But Incestuous Bastards: The Polemical Use of Sex and Sexuality in Hebrew Canon Narratives," in *Reading from This Place, I: Social Location and Biblical Interpretation in the United States* (Philadelphia: Fortress Press, 1995), 121–38.

16 Laura Donaldson, "The Sign of Orpah," in *The Postcolonial Biblical Reader*, ed. R. S. Sugirtharajah (Malden, MA: Blackwell, 2006), 159–70.

17 Graybill, *Texts after Terror*, 49.

18 Graybill, 52.

19 Susana Scholz, "Through Whose Eyes: A 'Right' Reading of Genesis 34," in *Genesis: Feminist Companion to the Bible*, ed. Athalya Brenner, second series (Sheffield, UK: Sheffield Academic Press, 1998), 171.

20 Musa W. Dube, "Dinah (Genesis 34) at the Contact Zone: Shall Our Sister Be Treated Like a Whore?" in *Feminist Frameworks and the Bible: Power, Ambiguity, and Intersectionality*, ed. L. Juliana Claassens and Carolyn J. Sharp (London: Bloomsbury, 2017), 39–58, 51.

21 Rachel Adelman, "Dinah: Bible," Jewish Women's Archive, June 23, 2021, https://jwa.org/encyclopedia/article/dinah-bible.

22 Rosemary Radford Ruether, "The Future of Feminist Theology in the Academy," *Journal of the American Academy of Religion* 53, no. 4 (1985): 704.

23   Renita J. Weems, *Just a Sister Away: A Womanist Vision of Women's Relationships in the Bible* (Philadelphia: Innisfree Press, 1988), 1, 2.

24   Graybill, *Texts after Terror*, 100.

25   Graybill, 112.

26   Nyasha Junior, *Reimagining Hagar: Blackness and Bible* (Oxford: Oxford University Press, 2019), 101.

27   Weems, *Just a Sister Away*, 7.

28   John W. Waters, "Who Was Hagar?" in *Stony the Road We Trod*, ed. Cain Hope Felder (Minneapolis: Fortress Press, 2021), 213.

29   Ken Stone, "1 and 2 Samuel," in *The Queer Bible Commentary*, ed. Deryn Guest, Robert E. Goss, Mona West, and Thomas Bohache (London: SCM Press, 2007), 195–221.

30   Graybill, *Texts after Terror*, 62.

31   Alexander Izuchukwu Abasili, "Was It Rape? The David and Bathsheba Pericope Re-Examined," *Vetus Testamentum* 61, no. 1 (2011): 2.

32   Graybill, *Texts after Terror*, 62.

33   Graybill, 78–80.

34   Pamela Cooper-White, *The Cry of Tamar: Violence Against Women and the Church's Response*, 2nd ed. (Minneapolis: Fortress Press, 2012), 29.

35   Trible, *Texts of Terror*, 5.

36   Trible, 46.

37   Trible, 46.

38   Trible, 45.

39   Trible, 46.

40   Graybill, *Texts after Terror*, 44.

41   Stone, "1 and 2 Samuel," 215–17.

42   Timothy K. Beal, *Esther*, ed. David W. Cotter, *Berit Olam: Studies in Hebrew Narrative and Poetry* (Collegeville, MN: Liturgical Press, 1989), 5.

43   Mark D. Roberts, *Ezra, Nehemiah, Esther, The Preacher's Commentary* (Dallas: Thomas Nelson, 1993), 447.

44   Elizabeth A. McCabe, "Defending Queen Vashti in Esther 1:10–12: What Her Attorney Might Say," in *Women in the Biblical World*, vol. 2, ed. Elizabeth A. McCabe (Lanham, MD: University Press of America, 2011), 35–51.

45   Beal, *Esther*, 8.

46   Elaine A. Heath, *We Were the Least of These: Reading the Bible with Survivors of Sexual Abuse* (Grand Rapids, MI: Brazos Press, 2011), 53.

47   Beal, *Esther*, 55.

48 Mona West, "Esther," in *The Queer Bible Commentary*, ed. Guest et al., 278–85.

49 Michael Carden, "The Twelve Books of the Minor Prophets," in *The Queer Bible Commentary*, ed. Guest et al., 446.

50 Carden, "The Twelve Books of the Minor Prophets," 447.

51 Renita Weems, "Gomer: Victim of Violence or Victim of Metaphor?" *Semeia* 47 (1989): 87–104.

52 Gerlinde Bauman, "The Just God as Sexual Predator," in *Feminist Biblical Interpretation*, ed. Schottroff and Wacker, 433–42.

53 Bauman, "The Just God as Sexual Predator," 439.

Chapter 7

1 Robert E. Goss, "Luke," in *The Queer Bible Commentary*, ed. Guest et al., 526–47.

2 Marcella Althaus-Reid, *Indecent Theology: Theological Perspectives in Sex, Gender and Politics* (New York: Routledge, 2001), 39.

3 Elisabeth Schüssler Fiorenza, *Jesus: Miriam's Child, Sophia's Prophet: Critical Issues in Feminist Christology* (New York: Continuum, 1994), 186.

4 Jennifer Garcia Bashaw, *Scapegoats: The Gospel through the Eyes of Victims* (Minneapolis: Fortress Press, 2022), 69.

5 James V. Garrison, "Casting Stones: Ballista, Stones as Weapons, and Death by Stoning," *Brigham Young University Studies* 36, no. 3 (1996–97): 350–62, 356.

6 Garrison, "Casting Stones," 357.

7 Elizabeth E. Green, "Making Her Case and Reading It Too: Feminist Readings of the Woman Taken in Adultery," in *Ciphers in the Sand: Interpretations of the Woman Taken in Adultery (John 7:53–8:11)*, ed. Larry J. Kreither and Deborah W. Rooke (Sheffield, UK: Sheffield Academic Press, 2000), 264.

8 Holly Yan, "Priest Abuse Victims Detail Lifetime of Trauma and Broken Trust," CNN, August 19, 2018, https://www.cnn.com/2018/08/15/us/pennsylvania-catholic-church-victims/index.html.

9 Trible, *Texts of Terror*, 1.

10 Graybill, *Texts after Terror*, 144–57.

11 Rebekah Legg, "Judges 19: Does the Bible Victim Blame the Women with No Name?" in *Map or Compass: The Bible on Violence*, ed. Michael Spalione and Helen Paynter (Sheffield, UK: Sheffield Phoenix Press, 2022), 112.

12 Tammi J. Schneider, "Achsah, the Raped Pîlegeš, and the Book of Judges," in *Women in the Biblical World: A Survey of Old and New Testament Perspectives*, ed. Elizabeth A. McCabe (Lanham, MD: University Press of America, 2009), 49.

13 Legg, "Judges 19," 114.

14 Deryn Guest, "Judges," in *The Queer Bible Commentary*, ed. Guest et al., 182–83.

15 J. Cheryl Exum, "Judges: Encoded Messages to Women," in *Feminist Biblical Interpretation*, ed. Schottroff and Wacker, 124.

16 US Department of the Interior Indian Affairs, "Missing and Murdered Indigenous People Crisis," accessed May 25, 2023, https://www.bia.gov/service/mmu/missing-and-murdered-indigenous-people-crisis.

17 Walker Percy, "The Man on the Train: Three Existential Modes," *Partisan Review* 23 (Fall 1956): 478–94.

Chapter 8

1 David Tombs, "Crucifixion and Sexual Abuse," in *When Did We See You Naked? Jesus as a Victim of Sexual Abuse*, ed. Jayme R. Reaves, David Tombs, and Rocío Figueroa (Norwich, UK: SCM Press, 2022), 16.

2 Tombs, "Crucifixion and Sexual Abuse," 18.

3 Pádraig Ó Tuama, "This Is My A Body," in *When Did We See You Naked?* ed. Reaves, Tombs, and Figueroa, 131–46.

4 Ada Maria Isasi-Díaz, *Mujerista Theology* (Maryknoll, NY: Orbis Books, 1996), 128–32.

5 Shanell T. Smith, "'This Is My Body': A Womanist Reflection on Jesus' Sexualized Trauma during His Crucifixion from a Survivor of Sexual Assault," in *When Did We See You Naked?* ed. Reaves, Tombs, and Figueroa, 278–86.

6 Rabbi Daniel Kirzane, "Understanding Biblical Sacrifice (Korbanot)," My Jewish Learning, accessed May 25, 2023, https://www.myjewish learning.com/article/understanding-biblical-sacrifice-korbanot/.

7 Kirzane, "Understanding Biblical Sacrifice (Korbanot)."

8 Yehuda Amichai, *The Selected Poetry of Yehuda Amichai*, trans. Chana Bloch and Stephen Mitchell (Berkeley: University of California Press, 1996), 156–57.

9 Monica Poole, "Family Resemblance: Reading Post-Crucifixion Encounters as Community Responses to Sexual Violence," in *When Did We See You Naked?* ed. Reaves, Tombs, and Figueroa, 67–90.

10 Poole, "Family Resemblance," 71–73.

11 "Report of the Independent Investigation: The Southern Baptist Convention Executive Committee's Response to Sexual Abuse

Allegations and an Audit of the Procedures and Actions of the Credentials Committee," Guidepost Solutions, May 15, 2022, https://static1.squarespace.com/static/6108172d83d55d3c9db 4dd67/t/6298d31ff654dd1a9dae86bf/1654182692359/Guidepost+ Solutions+Independent+Investigation+Report____.pdf.

Chapter 9

1 Matthew Fox, *Whee! We, Wee All the Way Home: A Guide to Sensual Prophetic Spirituality* (Rochester, VT: Bear & Co., 1980).

2 Audre Lorde, "Uses of the Erotic," in her *Sister Outsider: Essays and Speeches* (Trumansburg, NY: Crossing Press, 1984), 53–59.

3 Thich Nhat Hanh, "Mindfulness of Breathing 1," July 24, 1998, https://www.dhammatalks.net/Books2/Thich_Nhat_Hanh_Mind fulness_of_Breathing_1.htm.

4 Parts of this chapter were previously published in a short essay by Susan for Baptist News Global. Susan M. Shaw, "Celebrating Christmas with Extravagant Joy," December 15, 2022, https://baptistnews. com/article/celebrating-christmas-with-extravagant-joy/.

5 Kate Campbell, "See Rock City," Moonpie Dreams, 1997.

6 Victoria Safford, "The Gates of Hope," *The Nation*, September 2, 2004, https://www.thenation.com/article/archive/gates-hope/.

7 Paul Simon, "Graceland," Sony Music Entertainment, 1986.